4.3.78

Thomas Carlyle

University of Missouri Studies LXVI

Thomas Carlyle
"Calvinist Without the Theology"

Eloise M. Behnken

University of Missouri Press
Columbia & London, 1978

Library of Congress Cataloging in Publication Data

Behnken, Eloise M.   1947–
    Thomas Carlyle: "Calvinist Without the Theology."

    (University of Missouri studies ; 66)
    Bibliography: p. 142
    Includes index.
    1. Carlyle, Thomas, 1795-1881—Religion and ethics.
I. Series: University of Missouri—Columbia. University of
Missouri studies ; 66.
PR4437.R4B4   824'.8   77-11987
ISBN 0-8262-0234-9

To Creative Teacher-Scholars Along the Way

Acknowledgments

Alfred Lord Tennyson once had Ulysses say, "I am a part of all that I have met." In that sense this book is not my own but a melding of influences from many sources. As I look back over the years in which the ideas set forth in the following pages germinated, creative scholars stand out as direction-finders along the way. An enthusiastic teacher can express a thought in a way that opens up a new possibility, shifts your perception of the context, or changes your way of approaching the subject.

Half a dozen mentors and colleagues stand out in my memory as influential personalities, direction-finders. Francis Townsend opened my eyes to the rich diversity and vitality of life in Victorian England. The social issues of that era are still the unanswered questions of this century. For that reason Carlyle's writings provide clues to the solution of basic individual and social problems today.

Ralph McLain, John Priest, Frank Grubbs, and Leon Golden also fit into the category of notable professors. Whether the subject is biblical theology, classical comedy, or American history, each approached the topic as though it held the key to vital human questions. To have students read widely, dig into research sources, and analyze an author's basic understanding of life was their aim for the class. That approach makes learning individual, lively, and open ended.

To Albert LaValley go special thanks for answering a letter from a brand new Ph.D. whom he'd never heard of before. He graciously consented to read the manuscript, offered the initial encouragement to publish, and evaluated the book's strengths and weaknesses. His study, *Carlyle and the Idea of the Modern,* shed new light on the relevance of this eminent Victorian.

Thomas West, at a critical stage in the manuscript's acceptance for publication, invested much time and energy to meticulous criticism of stylistic and substantial matters. The book was much improved by such close reading and detailed comment.

Several typists have contributed to the final draft and to them I am grateful. Ms. Ann Shoemaker, Ms. Deborah Ronnie, Ms. Deborah Churchill, and Ms. Lisa Powell worked patiently with me to finish the project.

E. M. B.
Kansas City, Missouri
December 1975

Contents

Introduction

A social commentator once told a parable for our times. Two clowns, he said, were shuffling back and forth in the spotlight on a dark stage. They were looking intently at the floor and mumbling to each other, "Have you found the precious coin, the sacred talisman, yet?" As the minutes ticked by, one of the clowns realized that his partner was off in the dark, stumbling around, still searching. Came the question: "Why in heaven's name are you looking for the precious image in the dark where you can't see, you fool?" Came the answer: "Why are you looking for it in the light, since it is not there?"

The anecdote of the two clowns is a parable of religious uncertainty, the roots of which can be traced back to the nineteenth century. The Victorians had to face massive social changes brought on by the industrial revolution, the rise of the city, and technological discoveries; and in interpreting the meaning of these changes, they had to formulate a new vision of society and human existence. Thus, questions on value are dominant themes in the literature and art of the period as well as the theology and philosophy. In fact, the creators of literature were seen as a more reliable source of religious truths, at least by the intelligentsia, than the pulpit orators or doctors of divinity. Robert Browning, Alfred Lord Tennyson, Matthew Arnold, John Ruskin, Thomas Carlyle, and many other writers were considered powerful religious thinkers.

Thomas Carlyle, perhaps more than any other Victorian prose writer, saw himself as part of a literary priesthood and, in turn, was seen by his contemporaries as a prophet and priest. James Anthony Froude, in his biography of Carlyle published in 1884, chronicles the mission of his friend:

To those who enquired with open minds it appeared that things which good and learned men were doubting about must be themselves doubtful. Thus all round us, the intellectual light ships had broken from their moorings, and it was then a new and trying experience. . . . (Carlyle's words) to the young, the generous, to everyone who took life seriously, who wished to make an honourable use of it, and could not be content with sitting down and making money . . . were like the morning reveillée.[1]

Whether the image is of lightships adrift and lost or of clowns helpless and confused, the message is the same: every moral issue that had been considered undebatable in the past was debatable for the Victorians—something precious had been lost and no one could find it. This study explores the writings of Carlyle as contributions to the Victorian quest for belief. Its thesis is that Carlyle is far more radical than he is usually thought to be, for the world view he gradually builds and refines has much more in common with the death-of-God theology of the 1960s and 1970s than with the Calvinism he is often said to have inherited. Carlyle sought an anchor in the seas of change; he sought to redefine for his generation religious truths that could provide intellectual and emotional stability.

This study can be read as a consideration of Carlyle's response to what J. Hillis Miller calls "the disappearance of God" in Victorian literature.[2] Readers of Carlyle are familiar with the fact that he had once studied for the ministry, only to find that he lacked the convictions necessary for such a career. His choice of writing as a substitute for the ministry reflects his feeling that the religious truths for which people live and die are to be discovered outside institutional religion. God could not be found in the church, whether Evangelical or Anglican, or in a text from an ancient book. In a famous passage of *Sartor Resartus*, he wrote:

Meanwhile, in our era of the World, those same

Church-Clothes have gone sorrowfully out-at-elbows: nay, far worse, many of them have become mere hollow Shapes, or Masks, under which no living Figure or Spirit any longer dwells; but only spiders and unclean beetles, in horrid accumulation, drive their trade; and the mask still glares on you with its glass-eyes, in ghastly affectation of Life,—some generation-and-half after Religion has quite withdrawn from it.[3]

Another way of approaching this study is through a discussion of Carlyle's modernity in religious thought.[4] Ever since Bishop J. A. T. Robinson's *Honest to God* was published (1963), radical honesty has become a phrase that supposedly describes modern theological style. Of all the eminent Victorians, perhaps Carlyle was most rigorous in his attempts to cut away "sham" and "hypocrisy," terms he applied to anything that was not a product of direct human experience. Carlyle refused to follow the traditional dogma, seeking instead to find values that could be turned into a way of life. His skepticism, his honesty, and his insistence that values must be corroborated by individual experience mark him as modern.

A study of Carlyle's religious thought is at the same time an examination of his concept of history, or more particularly of the degree of control men have in the making of historical events. The chapter on work involves the role of man-the-maker and molder of his world. More broadly yet, it concerns Carlyle's understanding of human nature vis-à-vis God and historical circumstances. The discussion of the Hero is related to the theme of history in that the Great Man who appears at an auspicious moment can change the very direction of events, which implies a Promethean view of human nature. The analysis of eschatology and social theory is an attempt to determine the degree to which, in Carlyle's opinion, human beings can make their own world.

The general tendency of Carlyle's thought is to reduce the active role of God in history and the world and to increase the value of human activity. In a sense then,

Carlyle controverts mainstream Christian theology: from the story of the Garden of Eden to John Calvin's writings, the consequences of the cardinal sin of pride are clear. Pride, in the classic Hebrew-Christian sense, means setting one's will against God's will. Salvation, on the other hand, comes from humble submission to divine law. The crucial point is that human assertion and the divine imperative are mutually exclusive categories. Either man tries to "become like God," as Adam and Eve did, or he surrenders in true Christlike fashion, saying "not my will, but Thine." Carlyle, however, was unable to preach humility and submission. In his theory of work, his philosophy of history, and his view of human nature, he announces that the time has come for powerful men to act decisively in determining the direction of world events. In fact, Carlyle sounds more like a Karl Marx than a John Calvin.[5]

Although contrasts with traditional Calvinism should be evident in the following study of Carlyle's writings, a prefatory remark about the relation of the two needs to be made. A comparison of Calvin's works with Carlyle's would be out of place, in my opinion, because sixteenth-century Geneva bore little resemblance to nineteenth-century Ecclefechan or Edinburgh.[6] Thus, the great documents of Calvinism or the influence of rural Burgher Seceders lies outside the scope of this study.

In the past Carlyle usually has been considered a Calvinist in spite of the differences between his concept of salvation and that of Calvin. The most notable critic of Carlyle's religion, Charles Frederick Harrold, has set the general trend of the discussion of Carlyle's religion. He was convinced that in spite of the differences between popular Calvinism and Carlyle's thought, Carlyle was still, in the last analysis, a Calvinist. Harrold in his book, *Carlyle and German Thought,* states that Carlyle looked to German writers for new clothes for the old religion, but that his basic understanding of God and man was Calvinist in the traditional sense:

I hope, above all, that I have kept it sufficiently clear, throughout the discussion, that when Carlyle began the study of German writers, he already had a fundamental point of view, which he wished *confirmed,* and that he was "influenced" less by actual ideas than by the spirit of German thinkers as they clothed old concepts in new forms. Beneath the variations on the surface of his thinking, even throughout the years of his skepticism and despair, there persisted in him the essential spirit of Calvinism: the belief—at least the will to believe—in the infinite and transcendent sovereignty of God, to know and obey whom is man's supreme end. . . . As a "Calvinist without the theology," Carlyle sought, in German thought and elsewhere, an acceptable intellectual restatement of these beliefs.[7]

Harrold pursued his thesis further in an article entitled "The Nature of Carlyle's Calvinism."[8] He wished to demonstrate how much closer Carlyle was to Calvinism than to German influences. He chose four focal points: fatalism, a transcendent God, the elect, and irrationalism; and he showed how these points appear in Carlyle's writings, especially with respect to his social theory. Harrold's article concentrates only on the likenesses between Carlyle and Calvin, and his remarks have set the general trend of Carlyle criticism on the subject of religion.

Of equal relevance, however, are the differences between Carlyle and the Calvinistic tradition, especially with regard to the question of human salvation. A major point that stands out among all others in John Calvin's writings is that man cannot save himself, for in matters of salvation, men are completely in the hands of Almighty God. In the last analysis, according to orthodox Calvinism, human efforts to control individual and social destiny are insignificant. In order to be saved, men must surrender themselves to the grace and mercy of God, who alone is ultimately responsible for human beings, history, and all of creation.

The orthodox belief in God's active power and responsibility for salvation is the key point that reveals Carlyle's departure from this tradition. Carlyle puts the ultimate responsibility for history and human destiny squarely on men's shoulders, not on God's. Indeed, men, especially Heroes, are the principal actors on the world's stage, for they must govern the world and be responsible for it. The Almighty God of the Calvinistic tradition, the God of grace and mercy, has been replaced by an abstract, unfeeling, impersonal destiny in the face of which man is compelled to act heroically or be snuffed out. For Carlyle, man can and must save himself. And the challenge is to do or die.

Lest Carlyle appear as a complete eccentric in matters of religion, I wish to make clear that many Victorians shared his point of view. Carlyle only responded to the same social issues and pressures of psychological adjustment that his contemporaries faced, and in the process many of his questions were the same as those raised elsewhere by other artists. Arnold, for example, wrote poetry with the predominant tone of melancholy questioning and anxiety. The disillusioned, sad air is apparent in "Dover Beach":

> The Sea of Faith
> Was once, too, at the full, and round earth's shore
> Lay like the folds of a bright girdle furl'd.
> But now I only hear
> Its melancholy, long, withdrawing roar,
> Retreating, to the breath
> Of the night-wind, down the vast edges drear
> And naked shingles of the world.
>
> Ah, love, let us be true
> To one another! for the world, which seems
> To lie before us like a land of dreams,
> So various, so beautiful, so new,
> Hath really neither joy, nor love, nor light,
> Nor certitude, nor peace, nor help for pain;
> And we are here as on a darkling plain
> Swept with confused alarms of struggle and flight
> Where ignorant armies clash by night.[9]

Arnold had found himself alone and drifting in a world that supplied no rationale for anything. The world had become a "land of dreams," where each individual, with fear and trembling, had to work out his own meanings. The cosmos described in the poem is totally unfeeling, dark, and inhospitable. Carlyle described a similar world in his later writings.

This transmutation of the world from an expression of God's overflowing love into the world as a darkling plain involves an acceptance of historical change and consequent relativity. Arnold laments the loss of wholeness:

> Hither and thither spins
> The wind-borne, mirroring soul,
> A thousand glimpses wins,
> And never sees a whole.[10]

Part of the fragmentation comes from the realization that nothing is ever the same again. In the words of *The Rubáiyát*, as translated by Edward FitzGerald:

> Oh, come with Old Khayyám, and leave the Wise
> To talk; one thing is certain, that Life flies;
>   One thing is certain, and the Rest is Lies;
> The Flower that once has blown for ever dies.[11]

And because "modern man" experiences the moments running by and moving beyond his grasp, he is both the detached spectator and the impotent, indecisive human being. A voice in Tennyson's "Vision of Sin" calls us "Ruin'd trunks on wither'd forks, / Empty scarecrows, I and you."[12]

We are here today, gone tomorrow, and we seem to make no difference to the cosmic process. Arnold writes:

> What is the course of the life
> Of mortal men on the earth?—
> Most men eddy about
> Here and there—eat and drink,
> Chatter and love and hate,
>
> Gather and squander, are raised
> Aloft, are hurl'd in the dust,

> Striving blindly, achieving
> Nothing; and then they die—
> Perish;—and no one asks
> Who or what they have been,
> More than he asks what waves,
> In the moonlit solitudes mild
> Of the midmost Ocean, have swell'd,
> Foam'd for a moment, and gone. [13]

The world seems to exhibit a cosmic indifference that was never there in the days of belief in a personal, caring God. Those days, the Victorians worry, may be past forever. Although Tennyson's "In Memoriam" ends with a triumphant reaffirmation of faith, its early lines are full of questioning and fear:

> "The stars," she whispers, "blindly run;
>   A web is woven across the sky;
>   From out waste places comes a cry,
> And murmurs from the dying sun;
>
> "And all the phantom, Nature, stands—
>   With all the music in her tone,
>   A hollow echo of my own,—
> A hollow form with empty hands." [14]

FitzGerald echoes the same sentiments:

> And that inverted Bowl we call The Sky,
> Whereunder crawling coopt we live and die,
>   Lift not thy hands to *It* for help—for It
> Rolls impotently on as Thou or I. [15]

The situation is not that there is no cosmic order in the universe but that the order is no longer directly sustained by a caring, personal deity. God exists, but there is no longer immediate evidence that He does. He has disappeared in the sense that He is out of reach. Arthur Hugh Clough writes: "That there are beings above us, I believe, / And when we lift up holy hands of prayer, / I will not say they will not give us aid." [16] These thoughts are far removed from the sixteenth-century affirmation of Martin Luther, who is sure his God is a "Mighty Fortress" and a "bulwark never failing." God and man, nature and man, and man and man were once tied together, with lines of communication between them. But these understandings belong to a world view that is passing away, or that at least has been seriously eroded, by the nineteenth century. God seems to have withdrawn, leaving man with a sense of inarticulate loss and loneliness to fend for himself in a world "red in tooth and claw." FitzGerald says of the loneliness:

> There was a Door to which I found no Key:
> There was a Veil past which I could not see:
>   Some little Talk awhile of ME and THEE
> There seem'd—and then no more of THEE and ME.

> Then to the rolling Heav'n itself I cried,
> Asking, "What Lamp had Destiny to guide
>   Her little Children stumbling in the Dark?"
> And—"A blind Understanding!" Heav'n replied.[17]

In a significant segment of nineteenth- and twentieth-century literature, philosophy, and art there is, then, the recognition that something fundamental has changed in the relationship between God and his world. His disappearance is reflected in some of the major authors and works of the Victorian era. Carlyle, himself a worried man who abandoned his study of the ministry because he could not accept traditional creeds, was not immune from the widespread recognition that God was no longer present in the way He had once been. Carlyle, unlike Arnold, did not spend his time lamenting the fact of God's absence: instead he took the offensive and tried to reestablish a secure thought-world and a rationale for acting in the face of God's disappearance.

The Significance of Labor

"The end of a man is an action, not a thought" is one of Carlyle's oft-repeated statements. With elaboration, it could be considered the key to his interpretation of history, human nature, and existence. The concept of work will be explored in its relation to what Carlyle considered the problems of the age, the purpose of human life, the character of reality, and, finally, the way man, the history maker, relates to God. On this latter "God question" Carlyle is surprisingly modern; there are many similarities between his thought and an atheistic socialist philosophy like Marxism.

A beginning point for understanding Carlyle's idea of the character of the environment in which man lives is the inherent dualism that exists in everything—man, nature, and history. There are subterranean possibilities for good and evil seething in the heart of all things; and these contradictory possibilities exist in the same object at the same time. Carlyle often uses mythological terms to describe physical nature as two faced and unpredictable:

> Nature, like the Sphinx, is of womanly celestial loveliness and tenderness; the face and bosom of a goddess, but ending in claws and the body of a lioness. There is in her a celestial beauty,—which means celestial order, pliancy to wisdom; but there is also a darkness, a ferocity, fatality, which are infernal. She is a goddess, but one not yet disimprisoned; one still half-imprisoned,—the articulate, lovely, still encased in the inarticulate, chaotic.[1]

The fact that Carlyle sees both creation and destruction in the unconscious forces in the world not only appears explicitly, as in the above quotation, but also implicitly in the contradiction that is a part of his literary style and his treatment of historical events. Words compounded of opposites are characteristic of Carlyle's style. "Birth-death" of a new world applied to the French Revolution is an example. Literary images—the phoenix or the tree of life growing toward death—reinforce the notion of contradiction in the universe.

This understanding of inner forces was behind Carlyle's treatment of the French Revolution, for, in a sense, 1789 was a liberation of those forces that had too long been imprisoned in twisted, hypocritical traditions. The mobs portrayed at length in the first volume of his history represent these elemental forces; and they are described as floodwaters, volcanoes, fire, et cetera. They are the instincts of the French nation, a nation that has certain basic needs that are not being satisfied by the political structures. The mob wants bread, and it is willing to break all laws to get it. Its actions, like the storming of the Bastille and the rampage of the angry women ("maenads") become glorious moments in Carlyle's history. They are a release of elemental forces that have the possibility of regenerating French society. However, consistent with the concept of opposites existing in the same place at the same time is the final ironic outcome of this explosion of instinctual forces—the reign of terror and the incessant working of the guillotine. In Carlyle's view, there was a powerful demonic element contained in the creative instincts of the mob; and both good and evil came to be expressed in the final outcome of the French Revolution. There is, then, an opposition at the very base of existence; and whatever good appears, whether in physical nature or human action, is qualified and limited by the fact that it contains the seeds of its own destruction. Conversely, if it is destructive, it contains the possibility of becoming good. Carlyle is not given due credit for seeing the French Revolution as a positive good; he is too often accused of declaring that 1789 was

God's judgment on a sinful nation and that French society did well to uprise.[2] Actually, Carlyle treats the revolution in a balanced manner with plenty of attention paid to its positive and liberating aspects.

Carlyle questioned what this dualism means for man's work in the world. In common with the romantics, he believed in benevolent deity in nature, at least in his earlier writing (until 1848), and he implied that the inner contradictions in matter inevitably tend to work themselves out. All things are drawn toward resolutions; all things naturally "feel for" union with the totality. Carlyle's aesthetic theories have this notion of a divine eros attracting the mind to create, to assemble the bits and pieces into a design. In "Biography" he reasons that things become memorable because man both discovers and creates meaning for what he perceives:

> Often a slight circumstance contributes curiously to the result (of remembering): some little, and perhaps to appearance accidental, feature is presented; a light-gleam, which instantaneously *excites* the mind, and urges it to complete the picture, and evolve the meaning thereof for itself.[3]

The implication is that union with the all is a natural and even irresistible impulse. There is something in the universe that magnetically attracts the fragments around it; and the human mind, which is sensitive to this persuasive element in the world, is spontaneously drawn to clarity and resolution. There is another implication in the statement, however, which will receive more and more emphasis in Carlyle's later thought—the activity of the human mind as it imposes meaning on the fragments. In this quotation from "Biography" (1832) Carlyle is still willing to trust nature, for she is generally benevolent; but in his later writing (after 1848), she is full of deceit and trickery; and man must always be on his guard against seduction. In "Shooting Niagara: And After?" (1867) the mobs still represent instinctual forces, but these forces are to be subdued and repressed by military drill. But, for the early Carlyle at least, the inherent contradictions in matter will naturally work themselves out in coherent, and good, form.

The belief in spontaneous artistic creation, a widely held romantic idea, was probably what led Carlyle to see work in the positive terms that he often used to describe it in his early writings. Work is natural; it is simply the expression of man's instinct to make things. "He that works, whatsoever be his work, he bodies forth the form of Things Unseen; a small Poet every Worker is."[4] The phrase "body forth" is a capsule summary of Carlyle's aesthetic theory. The diffuse and formless naturally seek for embodiment, and in this sense we are all "makers," effortlessly.

Consistent with this theory of creation as bodying forth is the idea that man is a purposeful being who always has an end in mind. He is ever "on the way" somewhere. Man's inner impulses move outward with an innate sense of direction. While humans can consciously reflect on those ends and purposes, nature is unthinking and inarticulate. To say that man is an image-making, purpose-forming creature is also to assert his activity and control over the "dumb aspirings of his soul." He creates things, therefore, that mirror his own personality; and in this way, he humanizes the world around him; he makes a familiar nest for himself amid circumstances and raw materials not of his own making. Carlyle writes: "The world of Nature, for every man, is the Phantasy of Himself; this world is the multiplex 'Image of his own Dream.' "[5] Work as the expression of man's creative imagination lends a subjective quality to the surroundings because man makes things that are uniquely his. This subjective quality leads to emotional satisfaction both because man has something that belongs to him and because he is secure in what has become "home" instead of a hostile universe.

Carlyle's belief in the value of work bears a relationship to the religious problems of the age. One of the fundamental issues in the Victorian period was the erosion of traditional Christianity and the consequent spread of doubt and questioning. One writer put it: "The new world had no ultimate spiritual rationale. The old ethics and religion had no practical content."[6] Seen in this perspective the doctrine of labor became something akin to a religious feeling. It met needs that traditional Christianity no longer was able to fulfill when faced with the new conditions of urbanization, technology, the knowledge of man's power, and the necessity of reorganizing society. Labor, for Carlyle, became a practical answer to a pressing emotional need: labor gave people a sense of direction and accomplishment, a meaning in life. It became an end in itself to which all the fragments of life could be related.

Besides the positive aspects of work as spontaneous, creative, and yielding a sense of security and accomplishment, there is a more sinister side of the picture. As Carlyle got older, his attitudes toward life and society became more pessimistic, for example, in *Latter-Day Pamphlets* (1850). This distrust of nature and instinct can be seen as a logical outgrowth of the early belief in the inherent contradictions in matter. Although man perceives flux and incipient chaos in natural processes, he can be optimistic toward change if he is convinced that the movement is controlled by a benevolent force and that everything will ultimately work for the good. The facts of Carlyle's experience, however, simply did not bear out the trust that he had placed in the value of change, for society had not adopted his ideal plans for restoration (as in *Past and Present*, 1843); and he was not even making a financial success as a "literary priest." In fact, the application of ideas rather than force had not worked; and the whole concept of laissez-faire was badly in need of revision. He came to feel that decisive action was called for or England as a society would perish. The implication is that the inner contradictions, the demons, will end up triumphant if the process is allowed to flow on unchecked. Work, in this context, becomes a fight against chaos.

In *Past and Present* (1843) Carlyle often views nature as hostile. Work, then, becomes difficult; it becomes a battle. The issue is put in a mild form in "Characteristics" (1831), written even earlier than *Past and Present:* "Our being is made up of Light and Darkness, the Light resting on the Darkness, and balancing it; everywhere there is Dualism, Equipoise; a perpetual Contradiction dwells in us: 'where shall I place myself to escape from my own shadow?' "[7] It is significant that the light rests on darkness, that is, there is always the threat of chaos and destruction. At any time, the structures that man makes, the products of his labor, can turn into malicious and demonic forces that may devour the good he has created. We have now reversed the faith in a benevolent universe—instead of "from flux comes goodness," we have "from order and resolution comes evil." Man must continually be on his guard so that he is not seduced into idleness and a blind trust that all things work together for the good.

The idea of hostility in nature increases in Carlyle's thought as he grows older until he is using metaphors of hell for the world and images of battle for human life.

O Heavens, if we saw an army ninety-thousand strong, maintained and fully equipt, in continual real action and battle against Human Starvation, against Chaos, Necessity, Stupidity, and our real "natural enemies," what a business were it! Fighting and molesting not "the French . . ." but fighting and incessantly spearing down and destroying Falsehood, Nescience, Delusion, Disorder, and the Devil and his Angels![8]

Like Christian in *Pilgrim's Progress* man is called upon to struggle against the forces of evil. Life becomes a battle against Apollyon, an almost insuperable obstacle looming so large, blocking the straight and narrow path.

There is a modernity to the way Carlyle writes of the threat of chaos that perhaps puts him in the category with some of the atheists and blasphemers. He does not look to God for salvation; he looks to man. Over and over he repeats that laissez-faire in any sphere will not work. Individually, man must perform his duties well. Socially, he can and must steer political processes, and if he does not the whole world will go down in flames. Why does Carlyle de-emphasize the traditional role God plays in salvation? Perhaps it is partly because of his perception that the universe is pitted against men's efforts. The manifestations of primal power that we see are largely destructive. They are out to get man. These statements, given the Christian notion that God is responsible for creating the world, border on blasphemy, for they imply that God is not benevolent and He cannot be trusted. On the contrary, He has become his opposite in the guise of devilish forces. The only way out of the situation is to take up arms and do battle; man must look out for himself in a hostile world. Only man can ultimately be trusted; only man can wrest goodness out of the chaos.

Work, in this structure, becomes an attempt to subdue the chaotic forces and to keep them in their proper bounds. At an extreme, it becomes a personal fight with a malevolent force. This perception is modern in its implicit blasphemy. The fear that arises from living in an essentially hostile environment is also modern in the sense that there is a continual alienation in oneself, between people, and between the world and man. There is an abyss that is always present; we must act quickly in order to stay one step ahead of the void. Reality is "not there"; it has yet to come. "Understand it well, the Thing thou beholdest, that Thing is an Action, the product and expression of exerted Force: the All of Things is an infinite conjugation of the verb *To do.*"⁹ There is no noun, no substance, only verb and action; and the conjugation is never done; it is always coming, always future. Thus, the void of the "not" is always existent.

Carlyle's treatment of history also comes to grips with the "abyss of nothingness" because he greatly stresses the transience of historical forms and cultural institutions. After describing the collapse of French society he laments: "Alas, then, is man's civilisation only a wrappage, through which the savage nature of him can still burst, infernal as ever!"¹⁰ The destructive forces are there; and the "rinds of habit" are thin, but man must rebuild the structures even though they have a tendency either to explode or to dissolve in thin air. The alienation must be overcome or man cannot survive; so the continual pasting and patching, and sometimes the complete rebuilding of the wrappage, is part of man's labor in the world. He has to perform the task if he is to survive. A kind of desperation has replaced the feeling of security that went with work as artistic creation and humanization of the surroundings. Man must act even though he would like to "escape from his own shadow" to avoid facing the whole contradictory maze.

The relation of alienation to labor has an additional connotation. Labor cements relationships between people. One social doctrine on which Carlyle never changed his opinion is the belief that society at its best is an organic whole with all parts as "members of the body." A culture bound together by common meanings and roots, though, was his ideal. It came nowhere near describing England as it was, for society was actually split into aristocracy, middle-class Philistines, and the desperately poor. When one questioned the aristocrat as to what his work was, he could only answer "shooting partridges."

You ask him, at the year's end: "Where is your three-hundred thousand pound; what have you realized to us with that?" He answers, in indignant surprise: "Done with it? Who are you that ask? I have eaten it; I and my flunkies, and parasites, and slaves two-footed and four-footed, in an ornamental manner."[11]

Meanwhile, as Carlyle pointed out, the Irish widow was killing one of her children in order to use the burial fee to save the rest of her brood from starvation. Alienation between classes was a fact, Carlyle said, but sooner or later the rich would be forced to acknowledge the opposite of their original belief that they had no organic connections with other classes. When the woman with typhoid fever died and infected seventeen others around her, the human kinships could not be denied. Everyone must work together because the whole web would disintegrate if one part of it was neglected.

Labor, again, was the means of overcoming this antagonism between classes because it meant, first of all, that the aristocracy recognized a responsibility for the poor. They should be willing to bind themselves to the poor and, in economic terms, invest something in the poor by giving them a job. The work that the lower classes could do, given the opportunity, would give them a stake in society and the urge to see society prosper. The work that the upper classes could do would transform them into caring people who would also have a stake in the "poor question." Labor was the key to becoming a member of the body, according to Carlyle. Labor made each person worthwhile by making him matter to the general public. "Not a difficulty but can transfigure itself into a triumph; not even a deformity but, if our own soul have imprinted worth on it, will grow dear to us."[12] When we imprint worth, we become a community bound together by shared values. The excesses of Mammonism and unrestrained individualism could be overcome through work as caring for someone else.

Besides labor's value of making society truly communal and organic, it is also a making of cosmos out of chaos. Although this aspect of work is closely allied with life as a battle, it is important to describe more precisely what the struggle is against and what it produces in positive results. Disorder not only involves emotional instability and desperation, it can simply refer to the world in a raw state before man puts his hand on it. Notice what Carlyle uses as the opposing element in the following quotation: "Is not all work of man in this world a *making of Order*? The carpenter finds rough trees; shapes them, constrains them into square fitness, into purpose and use."[13] Physical nature is here not a force but an object to be molded and used by man to make his existence more comfortable. This is man against the wilderness; and the wilderness must be made into a Garden of Eden here on earth. For Carlyle, Frederick Wilhelm, father of Frederick the Great, is memorable precisely because he left some visible products of his reign. "He was essentially an Industrial man; great in organising, regulating, in constraining chaotic heaps to become cosmic for him. He drains bogs, settles colonies in the waste-places of his Dominions, cuts canals; unweariedly encourages trade and work."[14]

One of the significant elements that appears in this whole notion of turning the wilderness into a garden is Carlyle's continued interest in technology and its value in raising the standard of living. Given his denunciations of Mammonism, one might suppose that he disliked science and its hopes of making physical existence easier. However, Carlyle did not at all disapprove of advances in the standard of living. He preached against piling up wealth as a way of life, as a religion. He was also well aware that technology could make men mindless; it could turn into a machine that was capable of snuffing out human imagination; it could make men think they were cogs in a vast system over which they had lost control. Carlyle respected scientific advances because they were expressions of man's ingenuity and aggressiveness.

Carlyle was always sympathetic to the factory worker, his dreary existence, and his lack of power over his destiny. The sacredness of labor could be seen as an answer to this problem of monotony and loss of creativity, for Carlyle did hope to see that men be given meaningful work, although he had no practical schemes for changing the factory into a place in which men could use their imaginations. He believed that through his writing he perhaps could make men aware of their control over the environment, regardless of the encroachments of machinery. He preached the divine significance of each man in *Sartor Resartus* (1833) and, along with man's divinity, his ability to control nature and to steer the processes of history. "For man is not the creature and product of Mechanism; but, in a far truer sense, its creator and producer."[15] Again, the idea appears that nature is pliable under men's hands; and men's purposeful work can make of her what they choose, either a garden or a living hell, depending on their insight and forethought.

The belief that man is the crown of creation, the worker, producer, creator, is a fundamental theme in Carlyle's thought. In *Sartor Resartus* the German writer Novalis is quoted favorably to the effect that in every man is revealed a bit of the godlike. Furthermore, because matter is actually the divine "bodied forth," all that the workmen do is a revelation of the infinite. The Earth-Spirit in *Faust* says: "In Being's floods, in Action's storm, / I walk and work, above, beneath, / Work and weave in endless motion! . . . 'Tis thus at the roaring Loom of Time I ply, / And weave for God the Garment thou seest Him by."[16] Carlyle uses this quotation to point out that man is the master workman, whose actions constitute what is most real in the world, "so that this so solid-seeming World, after all, were but an air-image, our ME the only reality: and Nature, with its thousandfold production and destruction, but the reflex of our own inward Force, the 'phantasy of our Dream.' "[17]

quality of the total pattern is to focus o...
...rk as acts that matter, which make ...
...e universe.

..., and not sufficiently considered: how ...
...es coöperate with all; not a leaf rotting on ...
...but is an indissoluble portion of solar and ...
...s; no thought, word or act of man but has ...
...al out of all men, and works sooner or ...
...isably or irrecognisably, on all men![22]

...e take affects the nature of things; and this ...
...cause we live in an ever-changing, ever-...
...d. If reality for Carlyle, on the other hand, ...
...cribed solely as immutables or essences, ...
...be no room for qualitative change in the ...
...thermore, human acts would not ultimately ...
...undamental change in history, as it appears ...
...quotation, was an important part of Carlyle's ...
...f reality. Because things change, our works, ...
...ns make an imprint on the process. Part of ...
...ave done goes into the total stream of ...
...and changes its character. Nothing is ever ...
...d everything goes into the making of an ever ...
...lex universe. With regard to history, Carlyle ...
...e true Past departs not, nothing that was ...
...the Past departs; no Truth or Goodness ...
...man ever dies, or can die; but is all still here, ...
...nized or not, lives and works through endless ...
...The present is "the living sum-total of the ...
...st."[23]

...the kinds of statements that imply that man ...
...unforgettable mark on the character of reality ...
...works, we might begin to assume that man is ...
...ettered maker of history, the sole "world-...
...Man's work is a natural expression of his artistic ...
...s, a revelation of deity and a humanization of his ...
...dings. In all of these ways, man makes his own ...
...he other side to the notion of work as it appears

The striking point in this quotation is that man occupies center stage in a universe in which God is absent, and "ME" is the only reality. Man himself has become the definer of purposes, the "creator" of the world. This notion of God's absence from earth, except as we make Him present in our works, runs through a great part of *Sartor Resartus*, for after reading the book one of Carlyle's friends, John Sterling, complained that he could find no personal God in it. Carlyle replied, in effect, that any manifestation of "the divine" is not necessarily "The Divine":

> You say finally, as the key to the whole mystery, that Teufelsdröckh does not believe in a "personal God . . . ." A grave charge nevertheless, an *awful* charge: to which, if I mistake not, the Professor, laying his hand on his heart, will reply with some gesture expressing the solemnest *denial*. In gesture, rather than in speech; for "the Highest *cannot* be spoken of in words." "*Personal*," "impersonal," One, Three, *what* meaning can any mortal (after all) attach to them in reference to such an object? *Wer darf ihn NENNEN?* I dare not, and do not.[18]

Carlyle is appealing to the "God above God," for any creed, or naming, is blasphemy because it reduces the divine to a formula. This questioning of what we can know of the God who has disappeared marks him as modern.

Once God has been removed from the universe in such a way, however, human beings can see the divine presence in their own creations and works. We weave for God the garments we see Him by. This apotheosis of man, with its accompanying elevation of the natural to the supernatural, is one of the underpinnings of Carlyle's thought in *Sartor Resartus;* and it forms the substratum of his search for the Hero and his divinization of the labor of the common man.

The assertion that man replaces God needs a qualification. Although the tendency to deify man is certainly there in Carlyle's writing, he always stops short of a Nietzschean assertion that the Hero, or he himself, actually is God. Carlyle, unlike Nietzsche, has set up his interpretation of existence so as to make life essentially mysterious, indefinable. We might be symbols of the godlike; in fact, we might be all the divinity there is in the universe; but we are finite and limited. We float "on the æther of Deity"; we are "shadows flung out over the void." In other words, the Hero may function as God; but he is not the divine. In the same way, the products of our work may be all that can be revealed of the godlike, but the works are not all that exists in infinity.

This question of knowledge of ultimate reality is closely bound up with Carlyle's doctrine of labor. Work brings light and intelligibility into the world, as illustrated in *Past and Present* by the discovery of the true leader. "The clear-beaming eyesight of Abbot Samson, steadfast, severe, all-penetrating—it is like *Fiat lux* in that inorganic waste whirlpool; penetrates gradually to all nooks, and of the chaos makes a *kosmos* or ordered world!"[19] Samson, who took charge of the unruly monastery, plays God's role in Genesis 1: out of the void and darkness he brings light.

This light is not only order but knowledge of ultimate things, knowledge of the real character of the world. The sham and disorder have been penetrated; and the essence (or at least a symbol of the essence) has been uncovered. The work of Samson (whose name links him with the long-haired, powerful man of the Old Testament) reveals to him and to those around him what knowledge of the divine could be found in the world.

Carlyle's philosophy of labor answers one of the fundamental religious problems of the Victorian period—doubt. It is significant that he has not said that theological speculation or even new creeds are the first step in solving the problem of religious doubt. Carlyle's answer to a skeptical age was "work, and a real, in Carlyle's writings is submission to the eternal order of the universe, an order that man does not create but discovers. There is a criterion by which all works are measured and either found wanting or found sufficient: "the thing which is deepest-rooted in Nature, what we call *truest,* that thing and not the other will be found growing at last."[24] There is a cosmic pattern in the universe as a whole; there are established laws by which the world works harmoniously. Any violation of those laws will spell slow or violent death—but death nevertheless—for the organism that makes the attempt to break those laws.

There are a number of important elements in Carlyle's conception of existence as governed by transcendent law, the most important of which is perhaps that law, or cosmic pattern, denotes something abstract and remote. The processes of history and nature move on endlessly, but the law, or criterion, by which they are evaluated as good or bad is outside history and nature. It exists as a principle by which life is measured; it is the "ought" by which what "is" can be judged. However, Carlyle does not speak of a personal God who reaches down to us, interferes in history, and takes it upon himself to keep men in line with the "justice which is ordained from the foundations of the world," as it is put in *Past and Present.* Instead, the moral order is remote; it is closer to the inexorable workings of destiny than to the active, judging God of John Calvin. Teufelsdröckh would consider blasphemous the mention of a God who, in biblical terms, "walks in the garden in the cool of the evening." The personal deity is absent from the universe in the present age. This is not a fact to be lamented but rather it is progress, Carlyle believes. The sequence of ages in *Heroes and Hero-Worship* demonstrates what might be called the evolution of human consciousness. In the first lecture the Hero *is* God; in the second lecture he is the prophet inspired by God; then he is successively a poet, artist, et cetera. The movement is toward removing divinity more and more from the world, thus making room for a "higher" conception of God, that is, He is not the things in the created order: He stands above them.

> I should say, if we do not now reckon a Great Man literally divine, it is that our notions of God, of the supreme unattainable Fountain of Splendour, Wisdom, and Heroism, are ever rising *higher*; not altogether that our reverence for these (divine) qualities, as manifested in our like, is getting lower.[25]

God is absent from the world, Carlyle suggests with the notion of moral law, but He has left an orderly universe.

With God absent and only his imprint on natural processes left for us to read, the universe retains a bit of the mysterious. There are clues in the world as to what is required to live justly, but there are no definite blueprints; the world is written in hieroglyphics; and we must try to read its true meaning. The cosmic pattern is hidden and revealed at the same time because it is so remote and far off, yet discernible in nature and history, if man will just uncover it. It is intriguing to notice some of the ways Carlyle phrases the idea of interaction between a somewhat obscure moral order and man's activity, which is required to uncover the order and make it operative.

> Behind us, behind each one of us, lie Six Thousand Years of human effort, human conquest: before us is the boundless Time, with its as yet uncreated and unconquered Continents and Eldorados, which we, even we, have to conquer, to create; and from the bosom of Eternity there shine for us celestial guiding stars.[26]

The mystery and indefiniteness of the future are contained in "boundless Time" and "uncreated" continents; the revelation and certainty are contained in "celestial guiding stars."

The really striking point of these poles is that both are used by Carlyle to rouse men to work, to act. Precisely because the world is mysterious and man's final destiny is obscure, he must enter into the mystery wholeheartedly in order to discover for himself what is required of him and how he can be truly happy. Part of the "Everlasting Yea," or the way of salvation, lies in work:

> But indeed Conviction, were it never so excellent, is worthless till it convert itself into Conduct. Nay properly Conviction is not possible till then; inasmuch as all Speculation is by nature endless, formless, a vortex amid vortices: only by a felt indubitable certainty of Experience does it find any centre to revolve round, and so fashion itself into a system. Most true is it, as a wise man (Goethe) teaches us, that "Doubt of any sort cannot be removed except by Action." On which ground, too, let him who gropes painfully in darkness or uncertain light, and prays vehemently that the dawn may ripen into day, lay this other precept well to heart, which to me was of invaluable service: *"Do the Duty which lies nearest thee,"* which thou knowest to be a Duty! Thy second Duty will already have become clearer.[27]

One cannot see far ahead into the mysterious "uncreated" future, but he can see the next step; and if he takes it, the second step will become clear. Carlyle's world has more than a touch of mysticism; but the mystery is used to spur men to action; it draws them on and makes them seek a resolution.

The intellectual context of moral order and natural law is congruent with a rationalistic interpretation of the world, as well as the mystic one discussed above. Regularity and dependability are introduced in a universe where nature and history run by laws. Consequently, men can read the past in order to discover the patterns by which certain societies and men lived; and the readers can evaluate these patterns as to how much they produced in the way of "fruit." The best responses to life would have been preserved by history because they were in line with what ought to be. We can examine the ways of the past, then, in order to assess the present accurately and to plan for the future. This rationalism, or interpretation of existence as knowable, means that man has a certain freedom of action because he has foresight; he stands in a place from which he can examine the possibilities, relate them to his own situation, and then make his choice.

The theme of man's transcendence and freedom to choose occupies Carlyle's attention especially in the chapter on the "Everlasting Yea" in *Sartor Resartus*. It also is a fundamental premise of his social theory because he assumes that men can change societal patterns so that these patterns come closer to matching the cosmic one of justice. As for the individual, certain philosophies of the age have given him the impression that he is only an animal who seeks sensual pleasures. The greatest happiness for the greatest number had come to be the watchword of the day; and Carlyle disapproved of the Utilitarian theory. He continually satirized "gigmanity" with its complacent belief that respectability was derived from having a certain material standard of living; and he contemptuously asked if the Benthamites could grind virtue out of the cornhusks of pleasure. [28] All the patchers and quack medicine men in Europe were unable to make men really satisfied: "Will the whole Finance Ministers and Upholsterers and Confectioners of modern Europe undertake, in joint-stock company, to make one Shoeblack *HAPPY*? They cannot accomplish it, above an hour or two: for the Shoeblack also has a Soul quite other than his Stomach." [29]

What stands out in this passage is that although men exist amid certain necessities, their real happiness lies in curbing those desires in the name of higher needs and satisfactions. The answer to the question of how to find virtue lies first of all in renunciation of the endless seeking for more and more physical gains. ". . . *The Fraction of Life can be increased in value not so much by*

increasing your Numerator as by lessening your Denominator.
Nay, unless my Algebra deceive me, *Unity* itself divided
by *Zero* will give *Infinity*. Make thy claim of wages a zero,
then; thou hast the world under thy feet."[30] The purpose
of the renunciation is to restore autonomy to men. Once
they are no longer slaves to material desires, they can
choose much more wisely among the possibilities open to
them. They then can live in accord with "higher" desires,
those of the "Soul," because their autonomy and reason
have been restored.

Carlyle applies the same interpretation to society that
he does to the individual, namely, that the temper of the
times leads men to assume that they are controlled by
machinery not of their own making. But the key to justice
is not to remain in the bonds of established custom. Man
must break the customs and human laws in order to bring
society closer to the cosmic laws. Man should be in
control of the processes of history because he can know
its approximate true directions. He is the creature with
the vision to see the cosmic pattern; and he is also the one
to take those actions necessary to actualize those patterns
in his own society.

Carlyle's insistence on action, and man as the doer,
implies that God only sets up the ultimate standards—
He does not implement those standards. The implemen-
tation is man's work. In *Heroes and Hero-Worship* and
again in "Legislation for Ireland," the metaphor of the
plumb line and brick wall is used to describe existence.[31]
The remote moral order, the plumb line, is there and men
can see it. The raw materials, the bricks, are there to be
used. But the wall will not build itself. The plumb line
does not supply the energy, only the standard of
measurement. If anyone is to build the wall straight, that
is, reorganize social customs, it is man. He is responsible
for supplying the force that will determine the shape of
the wall; and the plumb line has been set in clear view for
him to measure his efforts.[32] If he fails, his blood is on his

own hands—he was not punished by an interfering, judging God but by the inadequacy of his own re- sponses. The French Revolution was brought on by men's failure to take care of the real needs of society; the patterns that were established were out of line with the natural order of the universe; and society exploded from its own internal pressures. God did not reach down from heaven to destroy the wall; instead the crooked bricks fell of their own weight.

Giving men the responsibility for forging the raw materials into a cosmos based on the proper patterns implies that men occupy a very important place in the total scheme of things. They are agents of fate; they become the master workmen who execute the remote designs of the universe. Perhaps they are not divine; but they certainly become heroic through courageously fac- ing the challenges of the world. The disorder that confronts man, then, has a positive value because it spurs him on to make it orderly. "Evil, in the widest sense we can give it, is precisely the dark, disordered material out of which man's Freewill has to create an edifice of order and Good. Ever must Pain urge us to Labour; and only in free Effort can any blessedness be imagined for us."[33] There are good aspects to the world, but the goodness exists as a promise, a not-yet. Goodness must be fashioned from evil, and the process is a difficult one. Our attitude must not be the mystic one of acceptance but the Promethean one of overcoming the hostilities of nature so that the good is brought out.

The greatest difficulties, when overcome, bring the greatest rewards. Notice the harsh obstacles that become stepping-stones in *Heroes and Hero-Worship:* "They wrong man greatly who say he is to be seduced by ease. Difficulty, abnegation, martyrdom, death are the *allure- ments* that act on the heart of man."[34] Hardship is the stuff from which Heroes are made: Samuel Johnson endured poverty and made his mark on the world of letters; Luther fought the whole structure of the Roman church and made a tremendous impact on history. The greater the challenge, the more resources must be called into play. That difficult times call for Heroes implies that hostile circumstances bring out the very best of which man is capable, requiring him to stretch himself to the utmost to overcome a great obstacle.

Besides calling up man's heroic instincts, obstacles have the added value of teaching us discipline, which is extremely important for survival in a hostile world. Otherwise, the challenges would overcome us. In Book 4 of *Past and Present,* Carlyle's admiration of military organization begins to surface. He sees the army as the only efficient and well-oiled institution in the present society. His whole plan of social regeneration involves "banding together" in a hierarchical structure, with each man submitting to the authority of those above him. By the time of "Shooting Niagara: And After?" (1867) Carlyle seems to be subordinating all factionalism, dissent, and "democracy," to recognition of law and order.

> I always fancy there might much be done in the way of military Drill withal. Beyond all other schooling, and as supplement or even as succedaneum for all other, one often wishes the entire Population could be thoroughly drilled; into coöperative movement, into individual behaviour, correct, precise, and at once habitual and orderly as mathematics, in all or in very many points.[35]

Effective labor will require submission to orders from above in the hierarchy, as evil teaches us the virtue of obedience.

There is something akin to irrationalism in Carlyle's thought, even though in some senses the universe is knowable and rational. In the concept of military drill, all honest seeking after truth, all criticism of the status quo, would be subordinate to the goal of human law and order. The extreme outcome of Carlyle's philosophy of action, with its consequence that practice is the criterion

of truth, is to subordinate interior and ultimate knowledge to efficiency and service. The tendency is in the
direction of ceasing to question what laws we obey and
simply to obey the laws that have been established by
custom or force. Especially in *Latter-Day Pamphlets* (1850),
the articles on the Irish question (1848), and "Shooting
Niagara: And After?" (1867), Carlyle all too easily identifies the order that men establish with the cosmic law of
the universe. And the powerful men, the "generals of the
army," become the judges of right and wrong.

Part of the reason Carlyle loses his original perspective
derives logically from his notion that men not only
discover "truth" but they also, by their actions, help
make it. The universe is not automatically sane and
dependable; but, rather, we must make it that way and
continue to keep it so through our efforts. "All works,
each in their degree, are a making of Madness sane."[36] In
the *French Revolution* he writes: "Man indeed, and King
Louis like other men, lives in this world to make rule out
of the ruleless; by his living energy, he shall force the
absurd itself to become less absurd."[37] Here we see the
will to control as an aspect of human existence: there are
raging, surging demonic forces all around us, and we are
compelled to impose order on those forces or they will
destroy us.

The order we impose involves a heavy emotional
investment on our part because any cracking of the
structure will compel us to redo the job, once again facing
all the risk of chaos. Thus, the high price put on human
law and order is perhaps why Carlyle is so fascinated
with the precision of military drill, where no disruptive
questions are asked. He does not want to face what might
happen if the man-made structures burst because the
result might leave the demonic elements in control. The
extreme psychological manifestation of this distrust of
everything around oneself is paranoia, the belief that
"everyone is out to get me." Of course, Carlyle was not

psychotic. Nevertheless, the hysteric quality of *Latter-Day Pamphlets* and of the articles on Ireland shows Carlyle's distrust and fear of any disruption of the laws that man has fashioned for himself from the insane depths. Especially in the pamphlets "Model Prisons," "Downing Street," and the "Stump Orator," he displays a total insensitivity to any point of view but his own. The world is not only insane and threatening, it is also filthy and disgusting. Carlyle feels no impulse to approach another tradition (see "Jesuitism"), or social class (prisoners), or any part of the world as it is except with a whip and gun. There is nothing that can be trusted except his own opinion, voiced in desperation. For example, the existing government has nothing by which to recommend itself; it can only be swept away by a Hercules. Downing Street is full of manure and needs to be cleaned like the Augean stables.

Carlyle worries that if force is not exerted by the right people, the whole rotten structure will cave in to suffocate everyone. The Herculean labor that the situation demands must be done if any sanity, cleanliness, or proper order is to be established. The Irish must be whipped into place and "purified" if they will not voluntarily submit to treatment. And if they are not cleansed, they will contaminate everything around them, including Carlyle and England.

> It is to ourselves also of the last importance that the depths of Irish wretchedness be actually sounded; that we get to the real bottom of that unspeakable cloaca, and endeavour, by Heaven's blessing, with all the strength that is in us, to commerce operations upon it. Purified that hideous mass must be, or we ourselves cannot live![38]

Work in this context becomes a desperate, last-ditch attempt to clean up an environment that has become unliveable. If the labor is not done quickly and forcefully, the diseased elements will inexorably infect those fairly healthy parts of society. The sentiment here, I think, is that the world is "out to get" us if something drastic is not done to remedy the situation. Carlyle has moved from man "can do" (because he is godlike, the master work-man, et cetera) to man "must do" or perish. Work becomes a perennial contest against almost overwhelm-ing forces working against us. And, as indicated before, part of the desperation comes from the belief that man, not God, is responsible for making a cosmos out of chaos. Man must impose his will on the disordered elements in true Promethean fashion; and, since the elements refuse to stay in place for very long, the battle must be a continual one.

Carlyle's disillusionment (in his old age) with slow, legal change in favor of drastic action by the strong man caused him to question the value of work in bringing about any fundamental changes in society or history. At times he seems to withdraw from any hope that labor is a means to any ultimate good. Rather, labor becomes an end that requires no justification: *"all* human work is transitory, small, in itself contemptible; only the worker thereof and the spirit that dwelt in him is significant."[39] Labor keeps men happy because it gives them something to do; but it accomplishes little outside itself.

Carlyle came full swing, from the optimism of *Sartor Resartus* and *Past and Present* to the desperation of *Latter-Day Pamphlets* and finally to the quiet resignation of his *Reminiscences* (published after his death in 1881). Whatever his emphasis, Carlyle's sights are always on man and his world, the challenges that make men heroic, the obstacles that spur them to be forceful, and the work on earth, which is perhaps all there is in the way of reward. Carlyle spends no time talking about God except as men make Him present in the world either by "weaving the garments" of divinity, or by playing the role of the master workman who orders the fragments according to a remote cosmic design.

In my opinion, Carlyle represents a new kind of humanism at the same time more pessimistic and more optimistic than Calvin was about man's possibilities for handling life well. Both of these thinkers see life on earth as a temptation and a snare; but for Calvin the snapping shut of the trap causes us to admit our own helplessness, throwing us back on God's mercy. For Carlyle the temptation has just the opposite effect, calling forth heroic actions as we pit ourselves against obstacles in order to remove them. In this sense Carlyle is more optimistic about man's ability to "save himself" than a Calvinist of the sixteenth century would be. In another sense Carlyle is far more pessimistic than a traditional Calvinist about human capabilities because Carlyle's God is a remote, inexorable, and unsympathetic destiny that will grind into the dustheap of history those who violate its laws. Man must act to make his individual and social living patterns accord with the cosmic *nomos*, or he will be extinguished by his own failure to act courageously and well. Hence, work is one of the fundamental parts of Carlyle's Weltanschauung.

Calvin, too, believed in the value of work, but part of the difference between the two thinkers stems from changed conceptions of reality from the sixteenth to nineteenth centuries. For Calvin, work was a discipline that enables one to enter the kingdom of heaven, beginning here on earth but continuing in a consummated and final form in paradise. Thus, for Calvin the real reward and justification of labor is in heaven. For Carlyle, however, the reward for work is in the here and now, in a changed earthly society. Hence, all his energy is directed toward the goal of letting all men live a full, complete human life in a regenerated social system. Heaven simply does not appear in his writing unless he speaks of heaven on earth. The implication is that if existence is justified, it has to be justified in this life. This emphasis on the earthly is especially evident in *Sartor*

Resartus, where he tells us that the supernatural is in the natural:

> Yes here, in this poor, miserable, hampered, despicable Actual, wherein thou even now standest, here or nowhere is thy Ideal: work it out therefrom; and working, believe, live, be free. Fool! the Ideal is in thyself, the impediment too is in thyself: thy Condition is but the stuff thou art to shape that same Ideal out of: what matters whether such stuff be of this sort or that, so the Form thou give it be heroic, be poetic? O thou that pinest in the imprisonment of the Actual, and criest bitterly to the gods for a kingdom wherein to rule and create, know this of a truth: the thing thou seekest is already with thee, "here or nowhere," couldst thou only see![40]

In a way Calvin could never be, Carlyle is a humanist and his focus is on man, his world, and an earthly reward. Besides deflecting attention from heaven, Carlyle removes the personal and active God of Calvin.

He turns what had been an anthropomorphic God into an abstraction—moral order—so that he can urge men to work. Although the personal God is absent, God in another sense becomes present in the secular by our works, as in the above quotation concerning the ideal in the actual. Again, the call is to work in order to weave the garments by which the divine presence can be manifested. Carlyle seems to be proposing a paradox: God is gone, so we must work; and God is here when we work. The important point is the heavy stress he places on human activity as crucial to the processes of history and world building.

Concerning the concept of a divine presence in the world, Carlyle, in large measure, erased the traditional separation between the sacred and the secular. One of the footnotes in Harrold's edition of *Sartor Resartus* defining natural supernaturalism is particularly instructive:

Carlyle's term denoting the real character of the world as he saw it: founded on mystery, a direct symbolizing of the infinite and eternal forces of truth and goodness, beyond the reach of our logical understanding, and therefore to be regarded with wonder and reverence. The age of ecclesiastical miracles has passed away; the old supernaturalism has yielded to a *natural* supernaturalism—all nature, as the revelation of God, is now sacred, and nothing is really secular.[41]

The "holy of holies" is right here around us, Carlyle is saying. Something significant is happening in the chapter on natural supernaturalism; and it provides the foundation for the early Carlyle's love of the earthly and human. The traditional demand for a choice between love of the world and flesh and love of heaven and the spirit has lost its force. Heaven and earth are no longer alternatives. They have been fused into God in the world, which, as Carlyle intends, leaves men with undivided allegiance. They are now free, able, and responsible for living their individual and social lives in such a way as to body forth the divine.

It may seem that Carlyle has made no real departure from traditional theological notions because he has, in effect, used both the idea of divine transcendence (removal from the world) and divine immanence (presence in the world). However, the creative contribution on Carlyle's part is the purpose for which he uses both the doctrines. No matter how he talks about divinity, the intention is to rally men to work. This humanism, with its primary energy directed toward man and his world, sets Carlyle off from traditional Calvinism.

Marx, a contemporary of Carlyle, could also be described as a radical humanist.[42] Although there are many differences between the philosophies of these two men, they share common conceptions of work. They both thought of labor as a means of overcoming alienation and as a way by which human beings build their world.

Marx believed that work, exemplified in the factory system, had become dehumanized. Money had become the standard used to measure the worth of what is produced; money had become the mediator between human beings.[43] With the advent of the industrial system, men found themselves condemned to pay homage to an external object, the pound or dollar, and as a result they become frustrated and alienated. Their satisfaction from creating something has been replaced by only an object, money. Capitalism and private property, Marx thought, make these conditions an actuality when ideally work should be an expression of creativity.

Marx distinguished between animality and humanity through man's ability to create and to work:

> The animal is one with its life activity. It does not distinguish the aim itself. It is its *activity*. But man makes his life activity itself an object of his will and consciousness. He has a conscious life activity.
>
> It is just in his work upon the objective world that man really proves himself as a *species-being*. This production is his active species-life. By means of it nature appears as *his* work and his reality. The object of labour is, therefore, the *objectification of man's species-life;* for he no longer reproduces himself merely intellectually, as in consciousness, but actively and in a real sense, and he sees his own reflection in a world which he has constructed.[44]

Marx and Carlyle agree in large measure on what sets men off from animals. Man is an image-making, purpose-forming creature who is always trying to make a home for himself in an alien universe.

For Marx, and to a lesser extent for Carlyle, man's labor makes an indelible mark on the nature of existence. For example, man invents a plow. The instrument has been fashioned by his own hands in accordance with an idea he had in his head. The plow is an expression of a subject, a person; but it is also an object that will, in turn, change the man's way of life. Because of what man has done, existence will never be exactly the same. Both Carlyle and Marx tell us that human acts matter, that they go into and change the living stream of experience. Man literally builds his own world.

Furthermore, man creates, or transforms his own nature as he works.

Labor is, in the first place, a process in which both man and Nature participate, and in which man of his own accord starts, regulates, and controls the material reactions between himself and Nature. He opposes himself to Nature as one of her own forces, setting in motion arms and legs, head and hands, the natural forces of his body, in order to appropriate Nature's productions in a form adapted to its own wants. By thus acting on the external world and changing it, he at the same time changes his own nature. He develops his slumbering powers, and compels them to act in obedience to his sway.[45]

Through work we mold physical nature and our own personalities; we develop our own potentialities and learn discipline.

Marx and Carlyle share an important similarity, too, in their understanding of what kind of universe we live in. The nineteenth century discovered a changing, evolving world in which flux plays a fundamental role. Because the world changes qualitatively, there is room for a concept of real human creativity such as Calvin never knew. In Calvin's thought, based perhaps on Augustine and ultimately on Plato, God is the unchanging reality who is both alpha and omega. The kingdom of heaven at the end of history was contained germinally in God's mind at creation. Ultimately, then, human acts, although they spell individual salvation or damnation, cannot change the character of reality. For Hegel, Marx, and Carlyle, however, the universe is a multiplex one in which things become their opposites in continual change, and any stasis is only transitory. There is room in a philosophy of flux for new creations as there is not when things are "predestined."

Predestination as it applies to an eternal God with an unchanging plan for creation involves the whole question of human freedom in history. Here again I think Carlyle and Marx work along the same lines, although the former would not go so far as the latter. The Marxist thinkers, in general, look at the Christian God who has the whole world in his hands and declare that such a divinity stifles human initiative and fosters feelings of helplessness. Religion is the "opium of the people." They then deny this God in the name of humanity. They say that the Christian tradition has demanded an either-or choice: either God and heaven or man and the world. They choose to affirm human creativity. Consequently, given the original choice, they are atheists.

Carlyle is less militant on the God question than the Marxists, but his position sometimes borders on atheism. He is unwilling to trust anything outside human action. His remote, impersonal God will not reach down to save us if we do not act well. We are responsible for ourselves; God is not. Certainly these thoughts go against the mainstream of orthodox Christianity, which has a deity full of grace and mercy. Both Carlyle and Marx are radical humanists who believe that human beings must save themselves and the world.

In conclusion, Marx and Carlyle shared much the same view of how human beings fit into the world of nature. Man fashions, molds, and creates objects that are expressions of his inner being. Through work humans produce themselves and their surroundings. Man is an "infinite conjugation of the verb *To do*."

To be human is not only to be active but to be aware of a momentous destiny. The earth and society must be reordered so that their design accords with cosmic justice. Only man can see the destiny and fulfill it. To rely on God, the radical humanists believe, is to pray for crutches or opium.

Carlyle's Early Heroes
Men of Ideas

"Understand it well, this of 'hero-worship' was the primary creed, and has intrinsically been the secondary and ternary, and will be the ultimate and final creed of mankind; indestructible, changing in shape, but in essence unchangeable; whereon polities, religions, loyalties, and all highest human interests have been and can be built, as on a rock that will endure while man endures."[1] Undoubtedly, reverence for Great Men is one of the keys to Carlyle's thought, but "hero-worship" is a simple phrase that covers a multitude of complex issues. Great Men make history, enlighten the world with their ideas, steer the processes of government, evoke religious devotion, and many other things. They change in shape, but their essential heroic quality remains constant. Somewhere between *Past and Present* (1843) and *Latter-Day Pamphlets* (1850), Carlyle's opinions about the role of Great Men and their relation to common people shift decidedly. Before that shift, Carlyle wrote of men whose ideas made them heroic. Those Heroes up to Cromwell, who marks the transition between the early and late Carlyle, will be treated in this chapter.

The complexity of hero worship gives rise to a number of questions. First of all, what are the characteristics of the Great Man? What is his function? How does he elicit support from society? What is his relationship to destiny, or God's will? In what sense does the Hero make history? And finally, how does he provide an answer to religious problems? We will explore Carlyle's answers to these questions by examining particular Great Men in rough chronological order as they appear in Carlyle's writing, including the essays on literary and political figures and the series of lectures, *On Heroes, Hero-Worship, and the Heroic in History* (1841).

There is a relationship between Carlyle's perception of the Hero and Goethe's concept of the distinction between Great Men and Noted Men, in particular, the criterion for measuring how heroic, or "great" a man was. One feature stands out as belonging to the Great Man: he transcends the spirit of his age. He has the sort of insight that puts him in touch with the wisdom of all time so what he says and does has its foundation in the bedrock of history. The Great Man stands alone; he is in a higher category than common men. The Noted Man, on the other hand, does not transcend the spirit of the time: "the Noted Man of an age is the emblem and living summary of the Ideal which that age has fashioned for itself: show me the Noted Man of an age, you show me the age that produced him."[2] The Noted Man is the "representative" one who mirrors the characteristics of his time; the Great Man stands beyond the zeitgeist, and in some way contradicts, or implicitly judges, the tendencies of the time.

This distinction between the Great Man and the Noted Man is important because it provides one criterion among many by which to decide whether or not a man is truly heroic. Some figures, even though they loom as large as Napoleon or Frederick the Great, are such heavily qualified Heroes that they become the best Carlyle can find, rather than the ideal for which he is looking.

Robert Burns, according to Carlyle, was "one of the most considerable British men of the eighteenth century."[3] Although born into a degenerate age of skepticism and trite literature, "he sinks not under all these impediments: through the fogs and the darkness of that obscure region, his lynx eye discerns the true relations of the world and human life; he grows into intellectual strength, and trains himself into intellectual expertness."[4] Burns wrote of rough Scottish life, but he did so in such a way that men could see the significance of the peasant world: "And thus over the lowest provinces of man's existence he pours the glory of his own soul; and they rise, in shadow and sunshine, softened and brightened into a beauty which other eyes discern not in the highest."[5]

Burns, then, has insight into the divine significance of the lowly. He is a sincere and honest man who writes from the heart, and in doing so he illuminates his small corner of the world by teaching others of the dignity of the common life. This quality makes him heroic.

Nevertheless, Burns, who takes "rank with the Heroic among men," had some serious deficiencies.[6] He lacked single-mindedness, "unity in his purposes, . . . consistency in his aims."[7] He had noble instincts, great potential; but he never accomplished anything world shaking because he was thwarted by his age: "in dim throes of pain, this divine behest (higher Truth) lay smouldering within them (Byron and Burns); for they knew not what it meant, and felt it only in mysterious anticipation, and they had to die without articulately uttering it."[8]

Burns was heroic insofar as he saw the "true relations of the world," providing light for others to live by as they watched his life unfold. But Burns was not the best of all possible Heroes because he could never fully express what he saw. His age did not understand him; indeed, it rejected him. Burns's actual work in the world appears small because, as Carlyle puts it, Burns had first to fashion the tools with which to work.

Just as Burns is one of the more considerable men in Britain, Voltaire looms large on the European continent. He is sometimes considered one of Carlyle's bêtes noires and therefore totally lacking in heroic qualities. Actually he is treated quite sympathetically more than once. The eighteenth century is devoid of real Heroes; but Voltaire and Frederick the Great are the best that the age can produce: "Friedrich and Voltaire are related, not by accident only. They are, they for want of better, the two Original Men of their Century; the chief and in a sense the sole products of their Century. They alone remain to us as still living results from it—such as they are."[9] So Voltaire certainly was a Noted Man—his influence was on a par with Frederick of Prussia.

Not only does Carlyle grudgingly admit that the famous Philosophe was a man of stature; but he links him with the third most momentous event in European history, the drama of the French Revolution.

> It may be said that to abstract Voltaire and his activity from the eighteenth century, were to produce a greater difference in the existing figure of things, than the want of any other individual, up to this day, could have occasioned. . . . Indeed like the great German Reformer's (Luther), his doctrines too, almost from the first, have affected not only the belief of the thinking world, silently propagating themselves from mind to mind; but in a high degree also, the conduct of the active and political world; entering as a distinct element into some of the most fearful civil convulsions which European history has on record.[10]

Carlyle's attitude toward Voltaire was ambivalent, just as it was toward the French Revolution because both were destructive and yet positive at the same time. Voltaire's admirable qualities have to do with his continual probing and question raising, his refusal to accept tradition simply because it was tradition. He is almost like Mephistopheles, that agent in the world who wills the bad and works the good. Voltaire lacked earnestness; he ridiculed and destroyed; yet "we may consider him as having opened the way to future inquirers of a truer spirit."[11] He was honest in a caustic way; and Carlyle, almost against his wishes, cautiously admired Voltaire's attitude.

Given Carlyle's respect for David Hume, one wonders whether he disliked Voltaire because of his skepticism or simply because Voltaire was a product of the French culture that Carlyle disliked. Hume and Voltaire were both skeptics, but Carlyle felt less suspicion of Hume's skepticism. [12] He enthusiastically recommended his histories to the family; and he thanked a school friend for sending a copy of Hume with: "I like his *Essays* better than anything I have read in these many days." [13] Again, in writing of the impact of education on Scotland, Carlyle has a good word for Hume: "It (the blossoming of thought) may utter itself one day as the colossal Scepticism of a Hume (beneficent this too though painful, wrestling Titan-like through doubt and inquiry towards new belief)." [14] These clues suggest that Carlyle objected less to Voltaire's skepticism than to his national origin.

The highest compliment that Carlyle pays to Voltaire is that the Philosophe "had naturally a keen sense for rectitude, indeed for all virtue: the utmost vivacity of temperament characterises him; his quick susceptibility for every form of beauty is moral as well as intellectual." [15] The Frenchman belonged at least in the circle of Noted Men; and he deserved the fame, for he did have some good characteristics.

Voltaire's flaw was that he lacked earnestness. He was superficial in his search for truth because he could only remove the first layer of sham; he could not penetrate to the mysterious all of the universe, as a true Hero could. His perception was limited to seeing logical coherence, arrangement; but he never found truth. [16] He was the *persifleur* par excellence. [17]

Samuel Johnson (Carlyle's essay on him was published in 1832) was an outstanding man for different reasons than the Philosophes; but he is still in the class of Original Men. Johnson's main characteristic was courage and a dogged perseverance in spite of poverty, public apathy, and personal misfortune. His life was an exemplum on maintaining one's integrity in the face of discouraging conditions. His biography preached that "Man is heaven-born; not the thrall of Circumstances, of Necessity, but the victorious subduer thereof: behold how he can become the 'Announcer of himself and of his Freedom'; and is ever what the Thinker has named him, 'the Messias (anointed) of Nature.' "[18] Johnson was resolute; and he had a deep respect for God and man. He was no mere ridiculer or *persifleur*.

Not only did Johnson keep the ancient faith in man's divine significance, he worked hard. He was a prophet: "the highest Gospel he preached we may describe as a kind of Moral Prudence: 'in a world where much is to be done, and little is to be known,' see how you will *do* it! A thing well worth preaching."[19] Johnson was a simple man of action, although the action was in a limited sphere. He started no revolutions, molded no cultures; but he had integrity and courage.

Johnson's writings, however, which should be his monument to posterity, are not of the best quality. "Into the region of Poetic Art he indeed never rose; there was no *ideal* without him avowing itself in his work: the nobler was that unavowed *ideal* which lay within him, and commanded saying, Work out thy Artisanship in the spirit of an Artist! "[20] He lacked the grand vision of the whole. He could not see beyond the "living busy world." "Prudence is the highest Virtue he can inculcate; and for that finer portion of our nature . . . where our highest feelings, our best joys and keenest sorrows, our Doubt, our Love, our Religion reside, he has no word to utter; no remedy, no counsel."[21] Johnson, then, had some heroic qualities; but he lacked the full stature of the Great Man.

The man to whom Johnson is being unfavorably compared in the above quotation is Goethe, who provides a catalog of the highest attainments of the Hero as literary man: "The history of his mind is, in fact, at the same time, the history of German culture in his day: for whatever excellence this individual might realise has sooner or later been acknowledged and appropriated by his country."[22] He was read by peasants and barons alike because his writings provided an essential recognition of what it meant to be a German; he could dig to the taproot of the culture. Anyone who had gone this deeply into one culture could also see the significance of man per se rather than simply man as defined by his nationality. Goethe had "gifted vision," "sympathy in the ways of all men." He was the "Teacher," "exemplar of his age" because he had learned how to live well.[23]

In Goethe a heroic characteristic appears that has not been evident in the figures discussed so far. He has *mana*, or vital power. "We say that we trace in the creations of this man, belonging in every sense to our own time, some touches of that old, divine spirit, which had long passed away from among us."[24] Goethe is set apart from us because he has access to a spirit we no longer can touch—except through him. He can play the role of the priest, mediating between the vital power and the people, bringing down the fire from heaven to give to men.

Goethe's life and writings contain many important lessons. He, like Johnson, was an autonomous man in the sense that even though he was immersed in his age, he could stand above it, separating its good influences from the bad and seeking out the best. Goethe determined, or fashioned, his own world:

> It was as if accident and primary endowment had conspired to produce a character on the great scale; a will is cast abroad into the widest, wildest element, and gifted also in an extreme degree to prevail over this, to fashion this to its own form: in which subordinating and self-fashioning of its circumstances a character properly consists.[25]

In Goethe's works we see "a mind working itself into clearer and clearer freedom; gaining a more and more perfect dominion of its world."[26]

There is nothing shrill or desperate in Carlyle's essays on Goethe, which were written between 1828 and 1832. The world, in these essays, is to Carlyle less like howling, mindless chaos and more like a garden ready to be worked until it is cultivated and can produce fruit. Goethe had a difficult task but not an impossible one. Once he had mastered the raw materials and had given them form, they stayed in place instead of continually collapsing into anarchy as the world threatens to do in Carlyle's later writings, like "Shooting Niagara: And After?" (1867).

Goethe's work was essentially creative, for he modeled a world out of malleable materials. By staying at the task, he succeeded in an admirable way:

> At one time, we found him in darkness, and now he is in light; he was once an Unbeliever, and now he is a Believer; and he believes, moreover, not by denying his unbelief, but by following it out; not by stopping short, still less turning back, in his inquiries, but by resolutely prosecuting them.[27]

The world can be made into a secure place. Man must be "gifted to an extreme degree" in an unbelieving age and must walk ahead calmly one step at a time working and cultivating.

How does Goethe accomplish the outstanding result of redirecting his life and culture? In these early essays Carlyle attributes the artist's success to the power of ideas, for the artist catches the people's imagination; they freely recognize his truth; and they follow gladly because he supplies the light for which they were searching. Goethe was an artist with a vision denied to others except as it is bodied forth in his life and writings:

> But this man, it is not unknown to many, was a Poet in such sense as the late generations have witnessed no other; as it is, in this generation, a kind of distinction to believe in the existence of, in the possibility of. The true Poet is ever, as of old, the Seer; whose eye has been gifted to discern the godlike Mystery of God's Universe, and decipher some new lines of its celestial writing; we can still call him a *Vates* and Seer; for he *sees* into this greatest of secrets, "the open secret"; hidden

things become clear; how the Future (both resting on Eternity) is but another phasis of the Present: thereby are his words in very truth prophetic; what he has spoken shall be done.[28]

The Hero as literary priest fulfills deep emotional and intellectual needs on the part of the people who follow him. He has the power to end religious doubt. The traditional vehicles of revelation, the institutional church and Scripture, had been all but discredited by the nineteenth century in the wake of the Philosophes and later the higher critics of the Bible. The intelligentsia could no longer accept plenary inspiration or its accompanying assumptions, and so the avenues for religious knowledge were limited in a way they had never been before. How could one know "revealed truth"? Furthermore, after the Deists with their remote watchmaker God, the question of whether "anything was up there" was disturbing.

The Hero as literary priest supplies an answer to religious doubt and the absence of a personal God. Carlyle is saying, as he discusses Goethe, that the sphere of the transcendent is difficult to touch and that it is not open directly to all men; but the wise and noble poet has access to it. Writing of Goethe he says:

> To our minds, in these soft, melodious imaginations of his, there is embodied the Wisdom which is proper to this time; the beautiful, the religious Wisdom, which may still, with something of its old impressiveness, speak to the whole soul; still, in these hard, unbelieving utilitarian days, reveal to us glimpses of the Unseen but not unreal World, that so the Actual and the Ideal may again meet together, and clear Knowledge be again wedded to Religion, in the life and business of men.[29]

Goethe, then, reveals in his life and writings the kind of truth that had heretofore been reserved for the church and Scripture. He bodies forth the unseen in the flesh; he

becomes a sign of transcendent wisdom. He not only
gives men clear knowledge of the divine but also moves
them to action, so that wisdom is "wedded to Religion in
the life and business of men." He mediates between the
divine and human like the priest, and he redirects men's
living patterns like the prophet.

Mention of prophetic elements in the Hero reminds us
that the Great Man often confronts the tendencies of the
age, standing in direct opposition to the status quo.
However, in these earlier essays, from around 1830,
Carlyle does not have the Hero working primarily by
confrontation and denunciation of the powers that be.
The literary priest does not level the structures, customs,
and institutions in existence in the name of a higher law;
instead, he re-creates the present structures on a higher
level. Goethe, as an Original Man, "stands above us; he
wishes to wrench us from our old fixtures, and elevate us
to a higher and clearer level. . . . For is it not the very
essence of such a man that he be *new*?"[30] In putting into
practice the vision of the literary priest, we must leave the
old behind and accept the new. Carlyle's Hero as literary
man does not carry a whip and gun or call upon an
efficient military machine to support his words. The poet
does not need an army because ideas will win in the
long run.

Another significant feature of Goethe's personality,
according to Carlyle, is that he was a sincere man who
appealed less to gentlemen, that is, "respectability,"
than to persons of head and heart. To speak of the heart is
perhaps another way of saying that Goethe called forth
certain feelings from his readers, feelings that were
inevitably attached to the man embodied in the writings.
The feelings were loyalty and admiration bordering on
awe because the Great Man exists apart in a sense. He has
a sacred mana that makes him mysterious and untouch-
able. He is even given religious names, like prophet and
priest, suggesting that he is in touch with the unseen
holy. Hence, his separateness and sacredness evoke

feelings of respect and devotion. He also calls forth trust from his followers because he provides security and a believable sort of knowledge, which fulfills emotional needs.

Because of this, men may transfer to the Hero as literary priest the feelings they had for God.[31] That Carlyle allowed Teufelsdröckh to get rid of a personal deity in favor of an Unnameable Almighty does not mean that he left the emotional satisfaction out of his "new religion" of *Sartor Resartus* (1833). On the contrary, the Hero, although he is not God, functions as the object or personality with whom we have rapport, communion. The Hero does for us emotionally what the now defunct (according to *Sartor Resartus)* personal deity used to. Goethe, the man and saint, is both removed from us and yet close insofar as he provides a higher model that we desire to imitate; but at the same time, the model is a human one, so we can have some confidence of living as he lived. He does not inspire so much awe that he is unapproachable; and he does not give us burdens that we are unable to bear.

All in all, the Hero as literary priest and prophet is a balanced, rational figure—rational in the sense that he continually seeks truth and never assumes that his answers are final, and rational also in that his ideas are subjected to the judgment of his followers. He elicits support by the inherent desirability of his thoughts; and if his readers do not find something in the Hero that is part of the "beautiful Wisdom," they simply do not follow or reverence him. The people judge whether or not his ideas matter. Apparently, at this early stage in Carlyle's thinking, he believes that even the masses can recognize a Great Man and can put his thoughts into action. Even the German peasants read Goethe because they are able to respect goodness when they see it. Later on, though, Carlyle's belief in the good sense of the common man, with its accompanying assumption that ideas need only to be known in order to be accepted,

gradually diminished. By the time of the Irish essays
(1848), he wanted the common people kept in line
forcefully because he saw them as stupid and anarchic.
Carlyle's conception of the kind of universe he lived in
also changed, from one in which persuasion and thought
could triumph to one in which bullying and force were
necessary. The world was no longer a garden to be
cultivated; it was a battlefield. And the Hero underwent
changes in the same direction: he became less the priest
and more the strong-armed man. The process of change
was a fairly gradual one, and it is more in terms of
changed emphases than of replacing one idea by
another. For example, Goethe, although primarily a man
of thought, was also a man of action; and Frederick of
Prussia, although primarily a man of practical affairs, had
a touch of the philosopher in him.

Some of the first men of action who interested Carlyle
were the outstanding figures of the French Revolution.
We begin with the Heroes from around 1837, Mirabeau,
and perhaps Danton, and move to the men in *Heroes and
Hero-Worship*. In the essay "Mirabeau" (1837), Carlyle
picks out a "questionable trio" of Great Men from
roughly contemporary times—Mirabeau, Danton, and
then Napoleon. Somewhat surprisingly, the first is
highly regarded, for Mirabeau is "of much finer nature
than either of the others," a much more "humane,"
"almost poetic" genius compared with Napoleon.[32] Why
is Mirabeau such a striking figure to the reader? One of
the obvious reasons is the vivid portrait of him by Carlyle:
whether or not the historic figure actually gave the
impression of great power is a matter for the historians to
decide. The man who appears in Carlyle's essay, however, is silhouetted against a background of elemental
forces. Even his birth is described like that of a demigod
sprung out of nowhere: "No stranger Riquetti ever
sprawled under our Sun: it is as if, in this thy man-child,
Destiny had swept together all the wildnesses and
strengths of the Riquetti lineage, and flung him forth as

her finale in that kind."[33] Mirabeau, of course, was of Italian ancestry, which explains the Riquetti surname. Carlyle's phrase for the family is "fiery Florentine."

The suggestion that Mirabeau belongs to a special race of men is enhanced by the imagery Carlyle uses all through the essay to describe the Great Man and his actions. The cosmic associations this man has are particularly striking. The metaphors used to describe him are almost all drawn from elemental forces. Mirabeau is like "red lightning," "fire," "volcano," "thunderbolts"; he is an "oak root," a "lion," a "wild giant." This Original Man has the same sort of elemental energy that Michelangelo portrayed in "The Creation" frescoes, where God passes the divine spark to Adam, awakening him to life. The analogy between Michelangelo's God and Mirabeau is quite close, for both of them have the kind of power that shocks everything around them into some sort of action.

Once the Hero is described in terms of elemental energy, the stage is set for seeing his life as a grand struggle to subdue the forces that set themselves up against him. Mirabeau's life is full of Promethean defiance and courage. He disobeys his powerful father and gets locked up in a stone castle for what he has done. He also loses all his money and his wife, but he never gives in: "The giant, we say! How he stands, like a mountain; thunder-riven, but broad-based, rooted in the Earth's (in Nature's) own rocks; and will not tumble prostrate!"[34] Nothing can overcome him, although he is punished for his defiance. Finally, his father frees him from the stone castle; and he is "hurled forth, to seek his fortune Ishmael-like in the wide hunting-field of the world."[35]

Elemental power and defiance are not Mirabeau's only mythic trademarks; he is of necessity destructive, too. Carlyle's favorite epithet for his Hero is "Swallower of Formulas," and we remember that Cronus swallowed his sons, all but Zeus, in order to do away with them.

Mirabeau refuses to allow the old order, with its hypocrisy and sham, to remain as it is. As a member of the
Third Estate, he defies the king's order to disperse and
helps to bring on the convulsions of the French Revolution. He destroys with a sweep of the hand or a word fitly
spoken.

An important characteristic of Mirabeau, besides his
strength and opposition to the present order is his
"veracity" and "insight." Because he is in touch with the
forces of nature he sees clearly. "This is no man of
system, then; he is only a man of instincts and insights. A
man nevertheless who will glare fiercely on any object;
and see through it, and conquer it: for he has intellect, he
has will, force beyond other men. A man not with
logic-spectacles; but with an *eye*!"[36] In contrast, Goethe's
insight—his faculty of seeing—came less from his breaking of crusts, of formulas, and more from his calm
penetration to the divine harmony behind the fragments.

Mirabeau is closely associated with destiny. From his
birth to his death, things sometimes fall into place by
chance. When the moment is ripe, Mirabeau happens to
be there. At other times, though, he is in the grip of stern
forces that "snatch" him away from his wife to send him
to Paris.[37] He seems a pawn, at times, on a giant chess-
board. At other times destiny is not nearly so purposive
as a chess game; destiny becomes accident, or the
roulette wheel; Mirabeau happens to be in the right
place at the right time. He defied Louis XVI; and the
Third Estate continued to meet:

> It is now that King Mirabeau starts to the Tribune, and
> lifts up his lion-voice. Verily a word in season; for, in
> such scenes, the moment is the mother of ages! Had
> not Gabriel Honoré been there . . . the whole course of
> European History (might) have been different![38]

It is a strange kind of destiny that has hold of Mirabeau
because it is not the kind of fate that is in the form of
moral law, laid out for anyone to perceive. Fate in

Mirabeau's life was unpredictable; or if there was a regular pattern to it, this Hero did not see it. Instead, the Swallower of Formulas acted by "instinct"; he jumped, so to speak, into the booming, buzzing confusion and worked out his destiny without actually perceiving the world-shaking nature of his action. He was an unpredictable giant, tied to elemental forces—forces like lightning that are unpredictable themselves. He struck fire when he acted decisively, when the moment was ripe: the kindling had been laid, and the Bourbon regime went up in flames.

It is also significant that Goethe, the literary Hero, had much more control over his life than Mirabeau, the Promethean Hero. Goethe created his world with his imagination as an artist; Mirabeau the lion chanced upon things to do. Mirabeau is like the summer lightning, which must crackle when the tensions have built up enough; Goethe is more like the rainwater that seeps through the earth and gradually forms crystals underneath. Goethe's ideas are most important; Mirabeau's acts are most important.

Mirabeau the monarchist receives far more attention and praise from Carlyle than Danton the Jacobin. What mention Danton does receive is quite favorable though; Danton, we are told, was a "Titan of Democracy" and a "friend of the people." He is similar to Mirabeau in character and appearance:

A rough-hewn giant of a man . . . whose "figures of speech," and also of action, "are all gigantic"; whose "voice reverberates from the domes," and dashes Brunswick across the marshes in a very wrecked condition. Always his total freedom from cant is one thing; even in his briberies, and sins as to money, there is a frankness, a kind of broad greatness. Sincerity, a great rude sincerity of insight and of purpose, dwelt in the man, which quality is the root of all: a man who could see through many things, and would stop at very few things; who marched and fought impetuously forward, in the questionablest element.[39]

Danton and Mirabeau were on opposite sides politically, yet Carlyle gives them both the supreme laud of
"sincerity," and sincerity, he tells us in *Heroes and
Hero-Worship*, is the primary characteristic of the Great
Man. Perhaps this admiration of Danton and Mirabeau
provides a clue as to why Carlyle groups such disparate
men into the single category of Hero. The implication
that emerges from the heroism of Danton and Mirabeau
is that heroism may depend less on what one believes
and more on how intensely one believes it.

Napoleon, as a Great Man of action, is classed with
Goethe in an essay Carlyle wrote in 1832. These two men
rank with the highest of all ages. In this essay, "Goethe's
Works," Goethe appears as a star, arching slowly over
the sky, whereas Napoleon is gunpowder, dramatic,
sudden, and short lived.[40]

Even though Napoleon had a "certain instinctive
ineradicable feeling for reality," an "instinct of Nature,"
he lived in the age of the empty Philosophes.[41] Hence, he
became a strange mixture of the quack and the true. His
good points are sincerity, feel for fact, belief in the career
open to talent, and the action he took to suppress
anarchy in France. Napoleon's early goodness later gave
way to fatal flaws, "false ambition," and "charlatanism,"
"believing in Semblances."[42] He began to trample on
others for his own gain, and the forces that he dominated
eventually lashed back at him, and he perished.

The next series of Great Men in Carlyle's writings are
the subject of the lectures of 1840 entitled *On Heroes,
Hero-Worship, and the Heroic in History*. The lectures dealt
with the Hero in six guises: divinity, prophet, poet,
priest, literary man, and king; and Odin, the Scandinavian chief god, was the first Hero of the series. Carlyle
devotes the greater part of his discussion of Odin to his
divine function rather than on characterizations of him.
Part of the emphasis on function is probably due to
Carlyle's own interests and purposes. All through the

series of lectures the function of the Hero remains a primary connecting link between diverse figures.

The first thing we know about Odin, says Carlyle, is that he was considered divine by the Norsemen. Although this assumption would be an impossible leap for men of the nineteenth century, it was a fact "earnestly true" to the primitive Scandinavians, for they lived in a universe whose prime quality was mystery. They believed that all natural things were invested with primordial power: fire was the god Loke; thunder was Thor; and frost was the giant Rime. The whole world was alive; it was, in Carlyle's words, "flashing, beautiful, awful, unspeakable."[43] The Norseman signified his intense awareness of mysterious force by giving divine, personal names to the things around him. He did not live in a world of objects but of personalities. He addressed his universe as "Thou," not as "It." Odin actually was a god to his people; and their natural response to him was awe, wonder, and more than a touch of fear because he was so unspeakably strange, full of mana. Odin as divinity was easily worshiped, reverenced, and marveled at by his culture. He supplied the dimension of the holy and awe inspiring for his people.

Odin also had a revelatory function, for he shined a light on obscure and diffuse elements and clarified them so lesser men could then easily see. He invented writing and poetry: "The rough words he articulated, are they not the rudimental roots of those English words we still use? He worked so, in that obscure element. But he was as a *light* kindled in it . . . and he had to shine there and make his obscure element a little lighter."[44] Like God, Odin separated the light from darkness and brought forth, for his culture, forms of definiteness from the confusing, inchoate void. Through him the Norsemen could see, could begin to perceive an intelligible world:

Has he not solved for them the sphinx-enigma of this

Universe; given assurance to them of their own destiny
there? By him they know now what they have to do
here, what to look for hereafter. Existence has become
articulate, melodious by him; he first has made Life
alive![45]

Odin brings form and intelligibility to the world; he
provides security by giving the Norsemen a familiar
universe in which their roles are defined.

In speaking of the Hero as providing clarity and light,
Carlyle is at least bordering on one of his favorite
themes, that of man's duty. Odin gave his culture
something credible—he satisfied their need for explanation of the world. Just as important, he gave them
something to live by and act upon. Although Carlyle says
high ethical content was not a part of Scandinavian
paganism, every religion must answer the question of
"what ought I do?"[46] Odin was the figure who united the
two issues of the true and the good, or knowledge and
ethics.

There is yet another facet of Odin the light bringer—he
is a pattern, a type. The future is of a certain nature
because he left his indelible mark on it.

Thus if the man Odin himself have vanished utterly,
there is this huge Shadow of him which still projects
itself over the whole History of his People. For this
Odin once admitted to be God, we can understand
well that the whole Scandinavian Scheme of Nature, or
dim No-scheme, whatever it might before have been,
would now begin to develop itself altogether differ-
ently, and grow thenceforth in a new manner. What
this Odin saw into, and taught with his runes and
rhymes, the whole Teutonic People laid to heart and
carried forward. His way of thought became their way
of thought:—such, under new conditions, is the history of every great thinker still. In gigantic confused
lineaments, like some enormous camera-obscura
shadow thrown upwards from the dead deeps of the
Past, and covering the whole Northern Heaven, is not

that Scandinavian Mythology in some sort the Portrai-
ture of this man Odin?[47]

The Hero as divinity is an archetypal model, an Original
Man. He is linked with the very roots of Teutonic culture
because his character made a difference to its identity. He
is the father. The Hero is with his people over their long
development not only as a memory in the past but also as
a continuing influence.

The Hero is a pattern in another sense, too, because he
is the summation of the inarticulate longing of a whole
people. Odin was the Original Man, "whose shaped
spoken Thought awakes the slumbering capability of all
into Thought. . . . What he says, all men were not far
from saying, were longing to say."[48] The Hero provides
the mirror that reflects all the unconscious impulses of
the culture as a whole. Through him the people can see
their desire and destination. They can get knowledge of
themselves through knowledge of him. He can provide
direction because they can see their existence clearly
when they look at him. The people follow Odin willingly
because they recognize him as fulfilling their needs; and
so the mimetic process is unbroken because it is uncoerced.

In the movement from the Hero as divinity to the Hero
as prophet, civilization has advanced a giant step,
according to Carlyle. Odin worship was actually a rude
kind of animism, with its belief in spirits and demons
inhabiting nature. The Scandinavians made no distinction between the god himself and that object in which he
manifested himself, whereas the Mahometan religion
had such a distinction. One of the basic truths that
Mahomet (who is Carlyle's example of the prophet in
Heroes and Hero-Worship) saw was that God was above
and beyond all nature and history and that everything
was utterly dependent upon his sustaining power.
Mahomet looked into the universe and penetrated its
secret:

> That this so solid-looking material world is, at bottom,
> in very deed, Nothing; is a visual and tactual Manifes-
> tation of God's power and presence,—a shadow
> hung-out by Him on the bosom of the void Infinite;
> nothing more. . . . At the Last Day they (the moun-
> tains) shall disappear "like clouds"; the whole Earth
> shall go spinning, whirl itself off into wreck, and as
> dust and vapour vanish in the Inane. Allah withdraws
> his hand from it, and it ceases to be.[49]

Because Mahomet was able to distinguish between
God and not-God, he could see the true significance of
the world of nature. He knew that things are not what
they appear to be; a burning bush is not just a burning
bush, nor, to make the mistake of the Norsemen, was the
bush actually a god. Instead, Mahomet could evaluate
the object in its proper perspective, as a manifestation of
and a message from Allah, who was above the bush, yet
who spoke through it. Mahomet the prophet had a
penetrating eye that the common man lacked because
Mahomet could strip off the wrappages and see the
object for what it essentially was.

All Carlyle's Heroes have this ability, like the prophet,
to see into the mysteries of the world.

> A Hero, as I repeat, has this first distinction, which
> indeed we may call first and last, the Alpha and Omega
> of his whole Heroism, That he looks through the
> shows of things into *things*. Use and wont, respectable
> hearsay, respectable formula: all these are good, or are
> not good. There is something behind and beyond all
> these, which all these must correspond with, be the
> image of, or they are—Idolatries; "bits of black wood
> pretending to be God"; to the earnest soul a mockery
> and abomination.[50]

Carlyle does not imply that Mahomet was a philosopher
in the tradition of contemplation and speculation. He
was a man of action who saw and was then compelled to
speak forth, to act, and even to make war in the name of
God's truth. A Hero cannot remain outside the hum and

bustle of things, contemplate, and find eternal reality. He must live fully and act boldly to discover truth. Carlyle insists that knowledge of ultimate things cannot be found without doing the truth. "To know a thing, what we can call knowing, a man must first *love* the thing, sympathise with it: that is, be *virtuously* related to it."[51] To Carlyle, virtuous relation had to do with duty, obedience, and hard work. Truth is not really apprehended until it is experienced. Mahomet was able to penetrate the world of appearances, not only because he had a quick mind but also because he had a "virtuous relation" with the universe. He perceived that all truth is essentially moral and he embodied that perception in his life and writings.

The sincerity of the Hero gives him an advantage that common men lack because the Great Man can appeal to a "higher law" to justify his actions. He has grasped a truth that is hidden to ordinary people; and in the name of that truth he can break the idols and formulas of his culture. He cannot live in sham because the "great mystery of existence" glares in on him and melts the wrappings away. He is compelled to act the way he does because Allah commands and he obeys.

In this progression, the Hero's link with inexorable destiny has been heightened from Odin to Mahomet. Part of this sequence is due, of course, to the nature of the religions of paganism and Mahometanism, since fate plays such a large role in the latter. Carlyle's emphasis on the Hero as an agent of Almighty God makes this quality an authentic mark of the Great Man. Mirabeau was made by the upper powers; and his life was a series of propitious accidents. Mahomet, too, is an elemental man. He had no formal education; his knowledge was from experience. He spends much time alone "deep down in the bosom of the Wilderness," and from nature he learns truth firsthand.[52] He is straight from the heart of the universe, "direct from the Inner Fact of things."[53] Mahomet, like Mirabeau, is also connected in Carlyle's writings with violent natural occurrences such as wind and lightning. He is "full of wild faculty, fire and light; of wild worth, all uncultured."[54] The Hero is connected with the inner heart of existence—he loves it, feels with it, and is moved to act by it. He is, in short, an instrument of the upper powers.

The other point that Carlyle heightens in his discussion of the Hero as prophet is the antagonism between the Great Man and the structures, customs, and institutions that exist. Mahomet had to be a man with a sword in order to accomplish his task because the mass of people laughed at him, with only a few following and trusting him. Whereas the Scandinavian people were eager to worship Odin, the Arabs were skeptical of Mahomet. Odin broke no formulas and upset no traditions as Mahomet did, but Odin had no need to use force because the divine mystery of the universe was an accepted fact in Scandinavian culture. Everyone shared the same interpretation of the universe. Divinity was close to everyone and everyone had fairly easy access to it, even though Odin was the supreme manifestation of mana and in that sense was removed from the people. In Mahomet's religion, contrary to Norse mythology, divinity was far enough removed from the masses that only the prophet could have access to it. Hence, the truth he saw was not apparent to them because the burning bush was god to them. They failed to penetrate the symbol and see it for what it actually was—a manifestation of Allah but not the god himself.

Because Mahomet saw a "higher truth" that is hidden to the common seeker, we have to take his word for it. In a leap of faith we yield to the prophet, abandoning our familiar psychological world and trusting that the new surroundings that the prophet reveals are better than the old. The breaking down of tradition is not easily or quickly done. Mahomet had to destroy to rebuild; and few people had the courage to follow the prophet into the unknown. As a result, we see that there may be hostility between the insightful Great Man and the common people who live by formula. Mahomet gave offense to everybody, Carlyle says, because he was an idol smasher, obedient to the will of Allah.

The Hero/prophet as an agent of God is, above all, obedient. He apprehends the truth, and he does it. Even though the world must become a battlefield because of the antagonism he arouses, he is compelled to go on. Thus, one of the best qualities a Great Man can have is courage, resolution. All of us are here, Carlyle believes, not to rest but to struggle and conquer: "It is not to taste sweet things, but to do noble and true things, and vindicate himself under God's Heaven as a god-made Man, that the poorest son of Adam dimly longs."[55] The Hero is not a humble character but a defiant one. He has to be in order to survive in a world that threatens to overcome him.

After the Hero as divinity and as prophet, Carlyle deals with the Great Man as poet in *Heroes and Hero-Worship*. The poet and prophet have the basic point in common of seeing through the vesture of things to the inner heart of them. However, whereas the prophet gives us a moral message, the poet's message is an aesthetic one. The poet does not preach explicitly so much as he simply uncovers truth in his artistic creations. Poetry is metrical, musical, according to Carlyle; and this quality, in the highest poetry, links the poetic thought to the great laws of the universe. "A *musical* thought is one spoken by a mind that has penetrated into the inmost heart of the thing; detected the inmost mystery of it, namely the *melody* that lies hidden in it; the inward harmony of coherence which is its soul, whereby it exists, and has a right to be, here in this world."[56] In this view, music and poetry are what Pythagoras the Greek took them to be—harmonies that echo the laws of the cosmos and reveal the origins of all things. The poet and the prophet have the same insight into the structure of existence, according to Carlyle.

Dante, the first poet dealt with in the third lecture, is memorable for at least two reasons: his intensity and moral earnestness. The words he wrote in *Divine Comedy* came out of the "hottest furnace of his soul."[57] His whole being was caught up in the endeavor to body forth the impulses that were burning inside him. Even with all this rushing intensity, though, the words of the poet were as carefully placed as the bricks in a straight wall must be. Dante did a beautiful job of constructing: each piece "answers to the other; each fits in its place, like a marble stone accurately hewn and polished. It *(Divine Comedy)* is the soul of Dante, and in this the soul of the middle ages, rendered for ever rhythmically visible there."[58] Dante was a master workman, doing no pedantic task but a sublime one—the task of visibly expressing his vision of the universe. He caught a part of the divine music of the spheres and rendered it forever memorable in his poem.

Dante had another quality that Carlyle admired. He was "not to be paralleled in the modern world" for his "rigour, earnestness and depth."[59] This stern Florentine did not weigh good and evil in a balance. He did not try to calculate how much good might exist in evil and vice versa. Instead he saw evil for what it truly was:

> Dante felt Good and Evil to be the two polar elements of this Creation, on which it all turns; that these two differ not by *preferability* of one to the other, but by incompatibility absolute and infinite; that the one is excellent and high as light and Heaven, the other hideous, black as Gehenna and the Pit of Hell![60]

Dante is like Mahomet in the certainty of his moral convictions; he is sure that "right is right"; and he is intractable on the matter.

Carlyle estimates Dante as stern and intolerant of what is unquestionably evil to him. This nonnegotiable quality is not only Dante's but also Carlyle's. He had an extreme distaste for the Benthamites who calculated virtue on a scale of pleasure and pain. In Carlyle's polemics against the Utilitarians, evil was intrinsically, and not instrumentally, wrong. Something was bad because it was by nature bad, not because of what it produced. In actuality, Carlyle's stress on works and practice nevertheless is closer to the Utilitarians than he would have liked to admit. We see that the Hero as prophet, poet, and later as priest is certain that his identification of evil is evil. One of his virtues becomes intolerance under the guise of moral conviction. The prophet and priest take decisive action to enforce their views. In Mahomet and Dante, then, we have come a long way from the calm faith of Goethe that his views can be set before men and accepted or rejected by the vast majority according to how well those views meet a felt need of the people. Perhaps Mahomet and Dante, whose writings appeal not to the masses, Carlyle says, but to the "pure and noble," live in a world where intolerance and force are necessary.

Shakespeare is the other poet discussed in the third lecture, and he represents something different from Dante. The medieval poet built a poem like a piece of architecture. In contrast, the Elizabethan one "grew" a poem unconsciously. Shakespeare's plays flowed "from the unknown deeps in him;—as the oak-tree grows from the Earth's bosom, as the mountains and waters shape themselves; with a symmetry grounded on Nature's own laws, conformable to all Truth whatsoever."[61] His unconscious vitality marked him as one of the great sons of nature, close to the inner workings of the universe. In this sense, he was original and authentic. Because he was in tune with the heart of nature, he had the insight to see through objects as though they were "windows on the Infinite."

Shakespeare was also a universal man, as Dante was not. Dante was "deep, fierce as the central fire of the world." Shakespeare was "wide, placid, far-seeing, as the Sun."[62] Shakespeare was perhaps not so intense as Dante, but he dealt with a wider range of subjects. In addition, he was universal because he articulated the great strivings of the English nation: what his culture unconsciously desired, he reflected in his writings, which gave his people an identity and commonality.[63]

Luther and Knox, examples of the Hero as priest (lecture four of *Heroes and Hero-Worship*) stand in somewhat the same relationship to one another as Shakespeare and Dante, for Knox was a man of much narrower abilities and interests than Luther.[64] Knox's only real talent was his capacity of "standing entirely upon truth."[65] He was a rough, sharp-tongued man of conviction, while Luther was a man of linguistic and philosophical talents, besides having sincere conviction.

According to Carlyle, translating the Bible into German or expounding Paul's letter to the Romans are Luther's side activities. He sees Luther first and foremost as a reformer. Luther was a revolutionary. He saw men in the sixteenth century as living according to outmoded formulas. Dante had no need to disturb the status quo because both he and his readers found Purgatory and *Malebolges* perfectly credible. Luther, however, lived in the sixteenth century, after Columbus had sailed to the West and discovered that Dante's mountain does not stand in the "ocean of the other hemisphere." The world view of the *Divine Comedy* was badly in need of revision by Luther's time: worship had become pretense. "Doubt has eaten out the heart of it: a human soul is seen clinging spasmodically to an Ark of the Covenant, which it half-feels now to have become a Phantasm."[66]

Because of the times Luther lived in, his task as he saw it was to do war against "Simulacra." His finest hour was when he defied the pope's authority with "Here I stand before God. I cannot go against my conscience." Luther called men back to reality by breaking outgrown idols and replacing them with ideas fitted to the changed times. He was a destructive man of necessity because the ground had to be cleared of rubble before a new edifice could be built. This revolutionary act took great courage and endurance, but in spite of the distrust and hatred of many Luther started a reformation of the beliefs of western Europe. He smashed the old structures, yet he provided direction for renewing them. A reformer-priest who molded new symbols by which men could worship the unseen, Luther reopened the channels by which men were united with their Creator: he was a mediator between the divine and human.

In *Heroes and Hero-Worship* there are fewer pages devoted to Knox than to Luther, probably because Luther broke the first furrow in Germany, while Knox followed to till the fields in Scotland. Carlyle's discussion of the two reformers makes them similar in character and function, except that Knox was a narrow man, and he was more persecuted in life than Luther. When Carlyle finishes with Knox the Hero, he has come close to describing a martyr. Everything worked against him. His society's reactions to him ranged from apathy to outright hostility and he lived in a time of war. "He bared his breast to the battle; had to row in French galleys, wander forlorn in exile, in clouds and storms; was censured, shot-at through his windows; had a right sore fighting life: if this world were his place of recompense, he had made but a bad venture of it."[67]

Carlyle uses the martyr-like elements in Knox's life to excuse his fiery rudeness. He had so much tribulation to put up with that he had to be a hard man; and his hardness was what made him memorable. He would have nothing to do with evil.

> He resembles, more than any of the moderns, an Old-Hebrew Prophet. The same inflexibility, intolerance, rigid narrow-looking adherence to God's truth, stern rebuke in the name of God to all that forsake truth: an Old-Hebrew Prophet in the guise of an Edinburgh Minister of the Sixteenth Century. We are to take him for that; not require him to be other.[68]

Carlyle avoids the issue of how right Knox was by emphasizing his noble purpose of establishing God's kingdom on earth.

History goes on, the old ages pass away, and along with it the ruder forms of heroism disappear. Even priests belong to the past, and in the nineteenth century Carlyle can find only two species of Great Men who are credible, the man of letters and the political ruler. In lecture five, the natural choice for the literary Hero would be Goethe, but because the German is virtually unknown to the audience, Carlyle chooses to describe Johnson, Jean-Jacques Rousseau, and Burns. These three, he carefully remarks, are "from a far inferior state of circumstances" to that of Goethe; in fact, they are not actually heroic.

> Alas, these men did not conquer like him (Goethe); they fought bravely, and fell. They were not heroic bringers of the light, but heroic seekers of it. They lived under galling conditions; struggling as under mountains of impediment, and could not unfold themselves into clearness, or victorious interpretation of that "Divine Idea."[69]

Because these men were unable to transcend the character of their times, they were unable to bring light to their readers. They could not stand beyond the zeitgeist, challenging it, breaking parts of it down, and reconstituting what they had destroyed.

Carlyle devotes half a dozen pages of lecture five to the impact that printing presses, the written message, and the lives and works of literary men have made in modern culture. Perhaps part of the reason for his reluctance to get to Burns, Rousseau, and Johnson is that they did not accomplish what a literary man can do ideally. The digression on the power of the written word is important in itself for understanding the Carlyle of around 1840. Even though the practical man of affairs, the king, merits a separate lecture, Carlyle is still speaking optimistically of the power of ideas. He lives in a kind of universe where in the free play of thoughts and opinions the best thought will inevitably win in the long run by its inherent virtue.

What the pulpit once did, the book does in the nineteenth century: "He that can write a true Book, to persuade England, is not he the Bishop and Archbishop, the Primate of England and of All England? I many a time say, the writers of Newspapers, Pamphlets, Poems, Books, these *are* the real working effective Church of a modern country."[70] Books are important because they meet a need for a modern age, the need to find something to believe in and to act upon. The audience feels the need, asks the questions; the literary artist responds with answers.

When Carlyle eventually begins a description of Johnson, the substance is the same as that of his essay entitled "Boswell's Life of Johnson." This man of letters endured poverty and distress but remained true to his convictions, which, however, were more practical than sublime. Johnson taught "Moral Prudence," moderation, and conservatism in all things. He was sincere not because he saw great truths but because he lived by the smaller lights he discovered.[71]

Rousseau is even less the Hero than Johnson. The Frenchman was "vehement" and "rigid" rather than "wide and deep"; he emitted more smoke than clear flame.[72] Furthermore, he was an "egotist" driven by vain ambition for money and fame. His portrait shows him to be a "Fanatic,—a sadly *contracted* hero."[73]

Two qualities redeem Rousseau; the first being that he was vaguely in touch with the true. He celebrated nature, and the savage life, an indication that he felt an awe before the mystery of the universe. The other quality that rescues Rousseau from obscurity is his intensity: "His Ideas *possessed* him like demons; hurried him so about; drove him over steep places!"[74] He was too intense for his feeble nature, and he was almost mad, but at least he believed in something.

Burns, the third Hero as man of letters, gets the same treatment as in the earlier essay on him. He was sincere; he discovered some sort of light; but he never could clearly articulate or even clearly grasp what he saw. And he was ruined by a skeptical age and the flock of admirers who lionized him.

In the lecture on literary men, Carlyle has not used the distinction between Great and Noted that he employed in "Goethe's Works"; but it does become evident that some Heroes are more heroic than others. Rousseau, Burns, and Johnson were not able to overcome the obstacles that confronted them. They endured; they did the best they could; but they lacked scope. Goethe was able to prevail over the chaos of the modern age, to fashion the elements into a new synthesis. "For Goethe has not only suffered and mourned in bitter agony under the spiritual perplexities of his time; but he has also mastered these, he is above them, and has shown others how to rise above them."[75]

In Goethe's transcendence of circumstances he inaugurated a new era in history. Goethe's life and writings supply the basis for hope. He brings in a new period in history because he teaches men "the worship of sorrow." He gives men new directions, and in doing so he moves history on a step. Goethe gave men practical operating principles.

The emphasis on action, duty, and practice is heightened in the last of the lecture series on Heroes in which Carlyle deals with the Great Man as king. He rises to ringing phrases about Cromwell and Napoleon—phrases that rather sharply contrast with those used for the literary men. It seems that Carlyle would like to think that ideas and books are a better solution than force and political leadership, but the situation is hopeless, considering that actual literary men fall short of the ideal. Carlyle calls for the literary priest, but the lecture shows that he is still waiting for more than one to appear.

In the sixth lecture of *Heroes and Hero-Worship*, only two kings are discussed, Cromwell and Napoleon. The latter falls short of the ideal because he degenerated from an admirable, powerful man to a vain, ambitious quack. Cromwell is a man of far higher caliber. In fact, he is so important that Carlyle devoted years of research to this Hero's letters and biography—research that issued in the writing of four long volumes published in 1845. It is to these volumes we turn our attention in the next chapter in an attempt to see what shifts appear in Carlyle's views on society, the Hero, and the common people. Cromwell is perhaps a transition between the Hero as man of ideas—Goethe being the best example—and the Hero as man of practical political action.

To Carlyle, all Heroes are intrinsically of the same stuff, only their mode of operation differs from age to age.[76] The elements of the heroic remain the same, but the degree to which certain elements are highlighted changes with Carlyle's developing ideas of society, human nature, and the character of the universe.

Carlyle's Later Heroes
Men of Action

There is a shift in Carlyle's views of social regeneration, the role of force, and the value of the common man, in his discussion of late Heroes. Great Men are no longer literary priests or philosophers but men of practical action. Even in the lectures on *Heroes and Hero-Worship* (1841), the Hero as king gets the high praise of being

> . . . practically the summary for us of *all* the various figures of Heroism; Priest, Teacher, whatsoever of earthly or of spiritual dignity we can fancy to reside in a man, embodies itself here, to *command* over us, to furnish us with constant practical teaching, to tell us for the day and hour what we are to *do*. [1]

The emphasis in this passage is on command and obedience and action. Find the able man, Carlyle is saying, and he will direct us in the wisest, fittest way. The assumption here is that the king not only will have power but also will have wisdom. Might and right will be united in the same figure.

Even though Carlyle says that the ideal leader has both wisdom and force, the emphasis on wisdom gets weaker and weaker, from *Cromwell* to *Frederick* to "Shooting Niagara: And After?" while the stress on power increases. By the time of the two Fredericks, all dissent is squelched, the powerful man is removed from the realm of criticism, and all barbarous acts are excused as foibles of an otherwise virtuous man.

Even in the 1841 treatment of Cromwell in *Heroes and Hero-Worship*, his power and energy are outstanding. He is made into the fierce warrior who has affinities with the elemental Mirabeau and the fiery Mahomet. This king is

> . . . the rugged outcast Cromwell . . . . The great
> savage *Baresark* (Berserker) . . . . He stood bare, not
> cased in euphemistic coat-of-mail; he grappled like a
> giant, face to face, heart to heart, with the naked truth
> of things! . . . I plead guilty to valuing such a man
> beyond all other sorts of men.[2]

Cromwell is a rugged giant; and his power catches
Carlyle's imagination as a part of the Puritan's essential
nobility.

That Cromwell was forceful few people would deny,
but that he was wise is a question Carlyle twists in the
manner of a demagogue who convinces his audience
through heavy-handed translations and substitutions.
Carlyle puts Cromwell in the "right" by denying any
merit whatsoever to the opposing side. In his estimation,
the seventeenth century in England was a grand battle
between Protestants and Catholics, which translates into
war between "Puritans" and "Ceremonialism," which is
really "Fact" against "Sham." If the opposing side has no
merit, then the consequence, of course, is that any
destruction of the opposition by Cromwell is justified
because he is destroying sham. Carlyle leaves the issue in
these stark black and white contrasts. Charles I was
beheaded and rightly so, says Carlyle, because he placed
himself on the side of hypocrisy, against the laws of
God.[3] Again, it was only just that Parliament abdicate its
responsibilities and resign its power to Cromwell because he knew God's will.[4] On another occasion, the
Puritan king dissolved Parliament because it obstructed
his plans for rebuilding the government.[5] Carlyle praises
this action on the grounds of its efficiency.

Regicide and the dissolution of the legally constituted
voice of the nation are momentous steps to take. If these
steps had been taken in the England of Carlyle's century,
one wonders what his reaction would have been. He was
terribly afraid of upsetting law and order in England, as is
evident from his fear of democracy (see *Latter-Day
Pamphlets:* "The Present Time" and "Parliament"). He

also described with horror what happened in France when a king was beheaded and power was in the hands of a ruthless few. Nevertheless, Carlyle excuses Cromwell's drastic action. Cromwell kills a king and makes himself dictator; and Carlyle has no censure, only admiration, for him. Something crucial happens in Carlyle's thought processes: there is a reversal of the issue of power and wisdom going on at least to the reader's eyes, if not to Carlyle's. It appears that what Cromwell does is good instead of Cromwell does it because it is good. Does Cromwell now make the law or does he continue to act within some sort of law? Of course, Carlyle would identify his Puritan Hero with the latter thesis, yet his description of him, in practice, fits the first thesis.

From Goethe, who freely earns his reader's respect through the intrinsic goodness of his words, we have moved to the man of practical affairs whose decisiveness leaves his constituency no room to question him. They are to submit to him and be obedient because God is on his side, and the Devil is on the opposition's side. The king becomes the agent of God in such a way that he comes close to being God himself. He is the creator of his own laws; thus in the name of a "higher law," he is outside any criticism.

> In plainer words, the original man is the true creator (or call him revealer) of Morals too: it is from his example that precepts enough are derived, and written down in books and systems: he properly is the *thing;* all that follows after is but talk about the thing, better or worse interpretation of it, more or less wearisome and ineffectual discourse of logic on it.[6]

This statement is from "Mirabeau" (1837), and although Carlyle would at times like to get around its sense by saying a Great Man cannot break God's laws and therefore cannot be unjust, the king worship he advocates circumvents the problem of justice by losing it in power. His true kings are beyond the realm of criticism because they are the "higher law."

There is irony in this reversal. The Hero starts out as an agent of a higher power; he ends almost completely identical with that higher power. The irony is so striking because in traditional Christian thought someone who usurps divine power is setting his will up against God. The supreme rebel was Satan. So, in the last analysis, although Carlyle would consider it nonsense, the Hero Cromwell plays a god or a devil, depending on one's perspective. Cromwell annihilates God insofar as he himself becomes the judge of good and evil.

Carlyle would never consciously push his Hero into playing either the Devil's or God's part; yet he assigns one of the mythic attributes of divinity to him in describing the man as possessed.

> Consider him. An outer hull of chaotic confusion, visions of the Devil, nervous dreams, almost semi-madness; and yet such a clear determinate man's energy working in the heart of that. A kind of chaotic man. The ray as of pure starlight and fire, working in such an element of boundless hypochondria, un-formed black of darkness! And yet withal this hypochondria, what was it but the very greatness of the man?[7]

It is strange that Carlyle recognizes the affinity be-tween the genius and the demon possessed, yet he still identifies Cromwell wholly with the "pure starlight."

The Hero of *Sartor Resartus* (1833) is wrapped in the same ambiguity. His very name links him with two opposite poles of reality: Diogenes meaning "God born," and Teufelsdröckh meaning "devil's dung." In speech he is also ambiguous, and the editor of the clothes philosophy wonders whether the utterances of the philosopher are the "Song of Spirits" or the "shrill mockery of Fiends."[8] Again, his eyes may be "reflexes of the heavenly Stars, but perhaps also glances from the region of Nether Fires!"[9] Carlyle in 1833 treats the principal figure of *Sartor Resartus* in a provocative, balanced manner, allowing the reader to make his own decisions about Teufelsdröckh's inspiration. Cromwell is not treated in a balanced manner.

This irony concerning men and objects is an integral part of Carlyle's view of existence. He dislikes logic chopping, with its presumption that causes and effects lie on the surface, easily accessible to the intellect. Instead, he believes that life is clothed in mystery, and, literally, that things are not what they seem to be. The Hebrew and his burning bush is a handy illustration, because Carlyle would agree that the bush is actually a vehicle for communication from the unseen holy. Appearances are deceiving; and when we penetrate to the core of a thing, we may find the reality to be the opposite of what we expected. This surprise reversal is linked with the Hero's role as "idol-smasher." He sees truth, which contradicts the appearance, the sham. Thus, fundamentally, the Hero, or seer, is a skeptic because he doubts what seems to be. At his best, the Hero is a seer who can penetrate to the heart of things and see truth. At his worst, he is a cynic who has no faith in anything but his own judgments and interpretations.[10]

The striking point, however, is not that Carlyle's writings show a recognition of the ambiguity in life and, indeed, continually use irony as a literary device, but that by 1845 and the Cromwelliad, Carlyle refuses to acknowledge that his Hero could be anything but God's elect. Reversals, indecisiveness, and lack of certain knowledge have perhaps become too great a threat to be admitted aloud. In the volumes on Cromwell, elements have polarized: evil is evil, and good is good. The real irony for the reader is that Cromwell has become the fountainhead of all that is good and that any questioning of his actions is blasphemous. Carlyle puts his Hero in the judgment seat, yet all his blustering does not convince the reader that God has the upper hand, rather than the Devil.

In *Cromwell* Carlyle also puts much less emphasis on the value of slow change through writers, books, and thinkers than on the value of revolutionary action. In his early essays, especially on Goethe, he argues that the literary priest's influence will far outlast that of the man of practical affairs like Napoleon. In his later writings Carlyle shows a disillusionment with books and ideas. In *Cromwell* he says that ideas and force are both essential; but the second must precede the first. Before there can be the free exchange of opinions, there must be law and order. When Carlyle has to choose between Shakespeare and Cromwell in 1845, the latter comes first because he must prepare the way. "As lightning is to light, so is a Cromwell to a Shakspeare *(sic)*. The light is beautifuler. Ah, yes; but until, by lightning and other fierce labour, your foul Chaos has become a World, you cannot have any light, or the smallest chance for any!"[11]

The choice of the man of action over the man of ideas reflects a change in Carlyle's notion of the character of reality, for what was once considered amorphous and perhaps even benevolent has now become chaotic and even malevolent. The earlier Carlyle assumed that Goethe's ideas would capture men's imaginations and that the common people would follow the literary priest voluntarily. The underlying assumption seems to be that the best thoughts can fend for themselves in the boundless jostle of life. In addition, Goethe is not strongly linked with destiny, a concept that suggests one way, the "right way," to do things, whereas the boundless jostle is a more open universe with various meritorious alternatives for acting.

In Cromwell's world the either-or alternatives are in clear and certain terms. Typical of the images used to describe the king's environment is that of the Hydra, whose hissing vicious heads are ready to poison the Hero.[12] In a world that is pitted against the Great Man, force is necessary.

One other consequence of Carlyle's interpretation of reality as full of hostile forces is that the Great Man must be responsible for his survival and also for carving out a small world in which to live. The hostility in the environment means that one cannot wait for salvation from above or he will be eliminated in short order. Instead, he must be aggressive enough to save himself. Furthermore, he cannot make the choice of the mystic to be passive and to "merge with the All" because in this case the "All" is poisonous. Thus, Carlyle's Hero as man of practical action must be a fierce character armed to do battle against the forces of evil. Because of the strength of the opposing powers, all his faculties are called into play; and he becomes heroic if he can overcome the threats of existence. He, not God, is responsible for his survival and for making his corner of the earth a cosmos in the midst of chaos.

Cromwell is a key figure between epochs, according to Carlyle, for he pushes history on to another stage as he sums up in his personality the strivings of his culture and as he directs it to better ways of doing things. Carlyle is convinced

> . . . that this man Oliver Cromwell was, as the popular fancy represents him, the soul of the Puritan Revolt, without whom it had never been a revolt transcendently memorable, and an Epoch in the World's History; that in fact he, more than is common in such cases, does deserve to give his name to the Period in question, and have the Puritan Revolt considered as a Cromwelliad. [13]

The Hero is the link between the ages; but he is not a static, passive figure who merely reflects the changes between epochs. Rather, he is bound up with the future, the age that is just arriving because he himself gives the next age its character; his personality leaves an indelible imprint on the nature of the times. History, in a fundamental sense, is epic because epics require dramatic conflict and powerful personalities.

Carlyle's treatment of Cromwell could be considered transitional because, at least in Carlyle's mind, the king's might is still inseparable from the right. The people recognize the truths for which he stands. They unite behind him in a Puritan revolt. In the later Heroes, though, the Great Man is in touch with a truth that is hidden to many. In fact, he must beat the masses to make them obey him. Carlyle also begins to lose the stress on right in the enhancement of power with the late Heroes like the military generals from "Shooting Niagara: And After?"

The last Great Man Carlyle names is Frederick the Great of Prussia; but the descriptions are laced with so many qualifications that we doubt whether Frederick deserves the title of Hero. Whereas Goethe was definitely Carlyle's literary priest par excellence, and Cromwell was the man of action par excellence, Frederick cannot be put in either category as a truly Great Man. Cromwell not only acted decisively but also saw the truth clearly, and he lived in an "age of belief." The Prussian king, though, was long on action and short on vision, making him less than the complete Hero. Frederick lived in an age of unbelief whose skepticism he never transcended, which was his real tragedy.[14] One remembers that Carlyle had the same problem with his recent Great Men in *Heroes and Hero-Worship*—Burns, Napoleon, Rousseau, and Johnson were potential Heroes, who were never fully heroic because the nature of the times defeated them.

All through the eight volumes on the history of Frederick, Carlyle suggests, either subtly or explicitly, that his Hero is not the ideal king; he is merely the best king in the eighteenth century. "Friedrich is by no means one of the perfect demigods; and there are various things to be said against him with good ground. To the last, a questionable hero; with much in him which one could have wished not there, and much wanting which one could have wished."[15] "My hopes of presenting, in this Last of the Kings, an exemplar to my contemporaries, I confess, are not high."[16]

Part of the problem with Frederick is that he is a tragic figure rather than an epic one. Whereas Cromwell achieved results that were unqualifiedly good, according to Carlyle, the outcome of Frederick's rule was a mixed blessing. The young Prussian had the best of the available education, but the best of an age of cant was Voltaire, who was Frederick's "chief Thinker in the world; unofficially, the chief Preacher, Prophet and Priest of this Working King."[17] The Philosophes were "deniers," not builders; they lacked real vision. Frederick acted according to the best lights available, but they were not good enough. The young prince, who fancied himself a philosopher and king, also considered himself a bit of a musician, poet, and man of letters. He even wrote a book called *Anti-Machiavel*. His policies were enlightened: when he ascended the throne in 1740, he opened grain supplies to the starving, abolished legal torture, insisted on freedom of worship and of the press, and established a "French Academy" of philosophy and science.[18] Nevertheless, Frederick's noble ideals were part of the cause of the French Revolution. Ironically, he was unaware that his permissiveness would contribute to such an upheaval. Frederick and the Philosophes could not see the consequences of what they were doing. The prince was a tragic figure who could not see far enough into the darkness; and the darkness eventually overcame him.

Another aspect of Frederick's failure, which is at the same time his success, is his decisiveness. At least, Carlyle says, he acted the best he knew how.

> But there is one feature which strikes you at an early period of the inquiry, That *in his way* (italics mine) he is a Reality; that he always means what he speaks; grounds his actions, too, on *what he recognises* (italics mine) for the truth; and, in short, has nothing whatever of the Hypocrite or Phantasm.[19]

Carlyle has not said that Frederick is in touch with the inner heart of truth; he has only said that the prince did the best he could under the circumstances. Frederick acted according to his interpretation of fact; but fact in the long run partly proved him wrong. The philosopher-king who had such noble and peaceful ideals for his country spent the greater part of his life at war.

Despite his flaws, Frederick's courage of conviction and his strong-armed policies were what gave him the potential for being a Hero. The militarism is what Carlyle admires about Prussia. Three of the eight volumes of *Frederick the Great* deal with events leading up to the actual reign of the king—it is the building of a Prussian military machine that has caught Carlyle's attention. The Hohenzollern dynasty was memorable because the rulers gave their people good, strong leadership, allowing no chaos or anarchy. They were governors who literally "steered" the culture by the stars of destiny. Apart from the Hohenzollern house, the exemplar drawn from the Hohenstaufens is Frederick Barbarossa, who acted in the same decisive manner, scourging the evildoers and aiding the well-doers.[20]

The most admirable figure in Frederick the Great's background was his father, Frederick Wilhelm. Since the latter gets the unquestioning approval Carlyle has heretofore reserved for Cromwell, one wonders whether Frederick Wilhelm is more heroic than his son. In our eyes Frederick Wilhelm deserves more than a little censure; but the very factors that destroy his image for the reader enhance it for Carlyle. Frederick Wilhelm was an "Industrial man" who drained swamps, settled colonies, and civilized the earth.[21] He was a worker, which anyone can admire. Less admirable were the means by which he maintained a force of superbly drilled elite troops who were "tall as giants." These men were impressed into service by Frederick Wilhelm's recruiting agents who roved northern Europe. They were kept in service by the threat of mutilation as punishment for any attempt to escape.[22]

Frederick Wilhelm gets Carlyle's admiration as an austere and upright man. He molded his son's character by beating and dominating him until the twenty-five-year-old prince attempted to run away from home. When he was captured, he was literally kept prisoner. One supposes this lesson taught him respect for his elders. Frederick Wilhelm was capable of slapping his daughter Wilhelmina in the face and of sentencing his son to death. The prince, after months of imprisonment, escaped his sentence by begging forgiveness from his father. Lieutenant Katte, an accomplice to the escape attempt and the prince's closest friend, was beheaded by Frederick Wilhelm's orders. Originally, the orders had been to stage the execution in front of the prince, but friends spared him from the spectacle. In all this, Carlyle emphasizes that force is necessary in order to run a state, and that Frederick Wilhelm acted according to fact.

> The soft quality of mercy,—ah, yes, it is beautiful and blessed, when permissible (though thrice-accursed, when not): but it is on the hard quality of justice, first of all, that Empires are built up, and beneficent and lasting things become achievable to mankind in this world![23]

For his brutality Frederick Wilhelm gets not censure but praise. Frederick Wilhelm taught his son what it meant to be a man. And his son certainly needed such strict guidance; Carlyle and Frederick Wilhelm would both agree. The crown prince was effeminate; he combed his hair in a French style; and he was off playing his flute when he should have been at drill. Even Carlyle fears that young Frederick's masculinity needed a bit of cultivating, although he dismisses the rumor of the prince's homosexuality as a calumny. At any rate, Frederick Wilhelm was certainly relieved to sever the friendship between the prince and Lieutenant Katte and the "French influence" by an execution. Carlyle believed that the father's stern measures saved his son's character.

Gradually the crown prince was forced to learn obedience, discipline, and submission to fact.[24]

The hardness and forcefulness that the prince learned from his father are the core of his admirable qualities. His prime goal was subduing the world through use of the grand military machine he had acquired. He spent the greater part of his life in a war that was unnecessary and even greedy. He wanted Silesia from Austria; and he misjudged the years of effort that were required. We find Carlyle excusing Frederick the Great just as he had excused the father and also Cromwell. The invasion of Silesia was obviously an offensive, not a defensive war, yet Prussia becomes in Carlyle's words "the First Nation of the Universe rashly hurling its fine-throated hunting-pack, or Army, of the Oriflamme, into Austria—see what a sort of badgers and gloomily indignant bears it has awakened there!"[25] The invasion was rash but glorious. Frederick the Great always lacked wisdom, but when he acted, he acted in a grand manner.

Carlyle has left the question of justice to fend for itself. In his treatment of Frederick the Great he has implied that in an age in which no one sees the way clearly, the answer is to jump into the jostle of things and hew something recognizable out of the chaos. Something is better than nothing, or the failure of nerve. The twin poles of justice and power have not been left to drift apart, but, rather, one has been merged in the other. What wisdom Frederick the Great had came from his willingness to act; he acquired knowledge by doing something.

Eric Bentley's comment on what he calls heroic vitalism describes the later Carlyle quite accurately.

> It announces an end to ideals, to the prescription of otherworldly ends, to the creation of double (Christian and Machiavellian) standards, and seeks to conclude the enmity in ethics of power and wisdom by locating wisdom precisely in the seizure and exercise of power itself.[26]

Frederick the Great's life taught him to put an "end to ideals"; and it taught him that bravery was better than humility. What Frederick lacked in wisdom, he made up by exercising his power.

However, a reading of the whole history of Frederick does not give the impression, as *Cromwell* does, that the king was more than mortal. On the contrary, his fallibility is emphasized all along—he never became epic in the manner of a Cromwell. Carlyle will only admit that the outcome was the best, under the circumstances, that Frederick could make it. Cromwell, on the other hand, made his own circumstances. Frederick, then, remains merely mortal, not an agent of God, therefore not able to take history into his own hands with a clear view of the consequences.

The Cromwellian aspect of the Great Man, his elevation to a demigod, gets combined later on with what makes Frederick great—his brute force—in Carlyle's most unflattering portraits of the Hero. In these portraits, which come from "Shooting Niagara: And After?" (1867), "The Nigger Question" (1849), and *Latter-Day Pamphlets* (1850), no man is actually named because the age is destitute of Heroes. All Carlyle can do is outline the things the man should do and hope that someone will step forth to save the day.

Although *Latter-Day Pamphlets* was published around 1850, its tone is quite close to Carlyle's writings of the late sixties, which intensify the tendencies seen in the Hero as strong man. Cromwell's world was rigidly divided into right and wrong, with the Hero on the side of right. Frederick's actions are justified simply because they come from a personality who "believes something." Just so, the ideal man of the later writings lives in a degenerate, putrid society in which any action is better than none. In the world of *Latter-Day Pamphlets* the enemy is inert, cast off, and not in the least a fit adversary. Thus, any means taken to cleanse the world are excused because the opposition lacks even the slightest vestige of dignity. The stupid people in "Model Prisons" should be beaten, locked up, and finally killed if they do not obey the "Laws of the Universe," that is, if they do not work. The worst treatment is too good for them, Carlyle says.

In *Latter-Day Pamphlets*, "Shooting Niagara: And After?" and "The Nigger Question," the Hero is entirely alienated from his surroundings. He is also wise insofar as he uses force because in a world of brutes, reasoning is ineffective. Carlyle does not even try to tie justice and power together except as justice becomes the use of the whip and gun to purge creation of its filth and filthy people. The accent falls on compulsion because there is absolutely no merit on the side of the opposition.

The Hero becomes God's vicar on earth; and whatever he says has been predestined from all time. Any refusal to obey the leader becomes blasphemy. In "The Nigger Question" Carlyle explains what to do when the native population refuses to work:

> In that case, it is full certain, he must be compelled; should and must; and the tacit prayer he makes (unconsciously he, poor blockhead), to you, and to me, and to all the world who are wiser than himself, is, "Compel me"! For indeed he *must*, or else do and suffer worse. . . . It was the meaning of the gods with him and with us, that his gift should turn to use in this Creation. . . . Yes, this is the eternal Law of Nature for a man.[27]

The Heroes (Goethe, Cromwell, Frederick the Great, and the military general) all have qualities in common but the degree to which certain elements are highlighted changes significantly for Carlyle. The Hero who looks into the inner heart of things is a skeptic in his own right because he refuses to accept appearances for what they are. This penetration is the reason Goethe was so great—he did not allow himself to be trapped in his own age. Mild distrust of appearances in Mahomet and Luther becomes "Idol-Breaking." By the time of the later writings, however, the "insight" has developed into complete cynicism accompanied by alienation and a refusal to trust anything but the Hero's own intuition.

The literary priest, Goethe, was authentic, an autonomous man who fashioned his own world from the diffuse raw materials. He was self-determined and self-directed. By the time of "Shooting Niagara: And After?" a personality that molds its own world, slowly and artistically, has become a military general who forces his will on everything around him because he fears his surroundings.

A world that was only amorphous, yet malleable in Carlyle's early writings, for example, *Sartor Resartus* (1833), has become a world that is full of deliberately malicious powers by the time of the later writings. The world is no longer a garden to be cultivated; instead it is a terrible jungle.

The early Hero, Goethe, supplies a primarily intellectual need on the part of the common man. He answers the question "What can be known of divinity?" now that God is removed from the world, for he bodies forth the unseen and is a sign of transcendent wisdom. Of course, for Carlyle the ethical question "What ought I to do?" is contained in the epistemological one. However, by the time of "Shooting Niagara: And After?" the common man is not capable of even asking a question about divinity, much less comprehending any subtle ideas. What was primarily an intellectual need ("What can I know?") has become mostly a practical question of "What must I do?" And one is not supposed to "reason why"; he is to "do or die," as the great master tells him.

Goethe could count on cooperation from the masses and a bit of help from the stream of nature, which culled out bad ideas and nourished the good in the long run. The later Heroes stand completely alone. Neither nature nor the common people can help them. What was once organic and cooperative now needs a strong-armed dictator to make it so. The Hero as man of practical action is left alone to bear the weight of the world on his shoulders. He lives in a barren world where no help comes from above or below.

The criterion used for judging the Great Man becomes practice and efficiency in the later Heroes. Frederick the Great accomplished things, whether or not they were "intrinsically right." Goethe, on the other hand, succeeded precisely because he was "intrinsically right."

The change in the configuration of the heroic elements reflects Carlyle's development during the forty years of his writing career. In some fundamental senses, the Hero as literary man is not the Hero as decisive actor in social affairs. What had been, in *Sartor Resartus,* a world in which men worked confidently to create order became, in the later writings, a world where order continually disintegrated. Man must fight desperately, without even knowing where he is going because the "celestial stars" are hidden to all but the elect, the Hero. And if the Hero is a Frederick the Great, even he has no real certainty that his reading of the "celestial stars" is accurate.

The literary priest and the king both perform the same psychological, emotional, and religious functions for Carlyle. The word *Hero* is Carlyle's secular way of saying "Christ," for when Teufelsdröckh rids himself of the God who walks in the garden in the cool of the evening, he looks for a substitution. Where is the link between the divine and the human if we think of God in a "higher way," that is, removed from the things in which He manifests himself? The Hero becomes the connective factor between God and man.

Goethe "weaves the garments by which we see God" in his life and writings. The artist creates and in the creation God is immanent. Thus, Goethe can reopen the channels of revelation between the divine and the human; he brings the godlike close to the common people as it had been in the Middle Ages. God is not remote from the artist; nor is He far from his people when the artist has done his work.

The key word, I think, which applies to the relationship between the artist, the divine, and the congregation is *participation*. Everyone's free and uncoerced response is called for, or the process will break down. The poet is necessary because his perception, interpretation, and creation leave their mark on the very nature of the truth that is apprehended. In Goethe, writes Carlyle, was the potential for inaugurating a new epoch of history, a new way to see, to believe. The literary artist becomes a Christ figure in the sense that his life makes a difference in the whole character of history. In other words, because he lived and created, things are changed. He provided a model by which existence could be reinterpreted; he provided a new foundation for faith.

The artist and the transcendent truth that he sees are not the only necessary "members of the body." The people's response to the man and his vision are vital, too. Goethe only bodied forth the heavenly wisdom—the choice of accepting or rejecting belonged to his followers. And Carlyle says that Goethe's truth was so compelling and yet so simple that even the peasants were charmed by him. They were caught up in the truths he presented because the vision satisfied their human need of finding something credible to believe in and act upon. The literary artist functions as the mediator between God and man, as the model by which existence is reinterpreted and as the personality who is both like and unlike his followers. He is enough alike to call forth feelings of love and devotion and enough unlike to be respected and loyally reverenced.

The possibility for artistic creation practically ends with Goethe's death; and the culture waits in vain for regeneration from the realm of ideas and books. The possibility of knowing divine truth, for all intents and purposes, disappears in the later writings of Carlyle. Frederick was a good man, but he was ignorant. If the king sinned through lack of knowledge, surely the common people lack the insight necessary to see God.

God changes from the creative, immanent Divinity to the judging one, the God of moral law. The later Heroes, like Cromwell, live in a world dichotomized into good and evil, and the Hero is identified with destiny. The king has become the sole agent for the God who is no longer evident in the world. There is no access to this divinity through literature or ideas; there is no possibility of knowing the deity except through radical and unquestioning obedience to the Great Man. Cromwell holds the keys to the heavenly kingdom, which no one may enter without his help. Cromwell plays the role of savior but not in a "graceful," caring way. The Puritan, and the God he serves, have become more like the inexorable fate that extinguishes the disobedient rather than the seductive and persuasive deity of the poet. Neither God nor Cromwell cares who lives or dies, so long as "Justice" is served.

The Hero as king provides, in essence, answers to religious questions. Where formerly we asked the poet "What can I know that I may be saved" we now ask "What must I do to be saved?" And the answer is "obey." Obedience to an able man, God's will in the flesh, is the key to salvation. Ethical problems are solved in a way. The emotions are satisfied, more or less, with a personality to reverence, fear, and worship. However, whereas we felt the artist to be human and kin, we acknowledge the king as more than mortal, and uncoerced love is replaced by awe and fear. The persuasion of the poet is discarded for the threat of hell's terrors and the actual terror of the Great Man's sword.

The Hero as poet or as king both perform the functions a Christ once performed; but they differ in type. Cromwell and the Heroes called for in the 1860s are not teachers or suffering servants; they are like the Christ who turned the tables of the money changers over and denounced the sellers and their "den of iniquity." Force used in the name of God is entirely justified, according to the late Carlyle. Indeed, power is a sign of the divine. It indicates conviction in an age of unbelief; and any conviction is better than none.

Carlyle in the 1850s and sixties thinks that there are no genuine poets in his day; that the common people are stupid: God is gone from his world; and everything has been sold to the Devil. Society will never be revitalized except through heroic action and the use of arms. Necessity, destiny, and moral law loom large in the writings of the later Carlyle; but man's desire to know and to do the good is gone. The answer is a strong king to whom we can turn ourselves over with relief. "The true liberty of a man . . . (consists) in his finding out, or being forced to find out the right path, and to walk thereon."[28] Freedom becomes recognition of necessity, being forced to walk on the "right path." All doubt is ended in submitting to the Hero. "So long as man remains free he strives for nothing so incessantly and so painfully as to find someone to worship."[29] The last sentence was spoken by the Grand Inquisitor, who kills the humble Christ in the name of necessity. Cromwell, like the Grand Inquisitor, puts an end to questioning and fulfills his culture's need for a source of authority and salvation. In the midst of threat, chaos, and malicious spirits, the Grand Inquisitor takes the humble Christ's place.

Eschatology and Social Theory

In Carlyle's later works, man, not God, has become the principal actor in the world, and we see the development of an extremely secular view of the final kingdom. A vision of "last things" involves justice—the attempt to make present living patterns reflect the cosmic patterns of paradise. Society and history are to conform to the universal nomos.

The question of eschatology embraces a number of issues. What is man's relationship to history? Does history have an end that is part of a predestined divine plan, unfolding without critical human participation? What is the relationship between the secular world and the transcendent kingdom of God? Is there regular and predictable progress in history? Are there cycles in history? The first section of this chapter will examine Carlyle's concept of "last things" through an exploration of these issues.

That Carlyle saw a pattern of cycles in the historical process can hardly be disputed, although the source of his idea of periodicity is uncertain. Hill Shine believes that Carlyle's notion of periodicity has a French source, the St. Simonians;[1] while René Wellek thinks the source is English or German.[2] There is conclusive evidence, though, that Carlyle did have a concept of definite cycles in the historical process. Some of the main grounds for making the conclusions are to be found in the series of lectures, *Heroes and Hero-Worship*. Carlyle tells us that four types of Great Men—divinity, prophet, poet, and priest—belong to bygone ages and cannot reappear in the modern period. "The Hero as Divinity, the Hero as Prophet, are productions of old ages; not to be repeated in the new. They presuppose a certain rudeness of

conception, which the progress of mere scientific knowledge puts an end to."[3] Besides the divinity and the
prophet, the world views of the poet (Dante and Shakespeare are the examples) and the priest (Luther and
Knox) are also outmoded. The only forms of hero worship for the nineteenth century are those of the literary
man and king. There are, then, "old ages" and "new
ages" in history, in other words, definite eras and cycles.

   Lectures on the History of Literature also presupposes a
pattern of rise and fall in the historical process. The first
period of literature begins with Homer and ends with the
Romans. Homer stands at the beginning of the period, at
the "ascent" part of the curve of rise and fall, because he
lived in a time of belief.[4] According to Carlyle, the apex of
the curve, or golden age, was from 445 B.C. to 345 B.C.,
with Euripides and Socrates marking the beginning of
the decline. These last two were incessant questioners,
deniers, unbelievers; they were symptomatic of a time of
"speculation" and introspection, which to Carlyle is
degeneration.[5] He does not explain why the questioning
exists, but he believes that introspection means loss of
vitality and consequent decline. The second period of
history begins with the Middle Ages and goes to John
Milton, when internal doubts and speculation again
mark a decline. The third cycle is the eighteenth and early
nineteenth centuries, which end with "Wertherism,"
that is, romantic discontent with no constructive outlet.
The potential for a fourth period of belief and vigor lay
with Goethe and has yet to bloom. History, then, has a
pattern of ascent, culmination, and descent.

   Given a definite concept of periodicity, we may ask
whether or not the process is regular, working by
discernible and predictable laws. Several ideas in Carlyle's writing militate against any notion of regularity in
the historical process. He heavily emphasizes the individuality of each period and national culture, seeing in
each period a certain "physiognomy" that belongs to no
other.[6] In a statement making parallel the uniqueness of a

personality and the uniqueness of a nation or an era, Carlyle writes:

> For the great law of culture is: Let each become all that he was created capable of being; expand, if possible, to his full growth; resisting all impediments, casting off all foreign, especially all noxious adhesions; and show himself at length in his own shape and stature, be these what they may. There is no uniform of excellence either in physical or spiritual Nature: all *genuine* things are what they ought to be.[7]

Carlyle balanced the notion of uniqueness and individuality with commonality: he wrote biographies with the assumption that general lessons could be learned from one person's life.

Another Carlylean assumption that reduces predictability in history is that of the apocalyptic nature of social change. One has only to read the *French Revolution* to be impressed by Carlyle's description of the immense surging energy in the world and its volcanic destruction. Without forewarning, the revolutionary pressures gradually built up to overthrow the French government. "Smoke as of Tophet; confusion as of Babel; noise as of the Crack of Doom!"[8] This statement is a description of vast upheaval and rending of the social fabric, not of slow, evolutionary change by regular laws of history. Anyone could see, in retrospect, that the conditions for revolution were present; but no one could tell the hour of the "Death-Birth of a New World"; and no one could foresee all the consequences of the actions taken by the mobs and the leaders.

Carlyle's hero worship adds to the unpredictability of historical change. We are told that the lion-voiced Mirabeau appeared in the Third Estate at precisely the ripe moment and changed the course of European history. If he had not been there, the outcome would have been vastly different. The Great Man of *Heroes and Hero-Worship* impresses his character on historical events;

the stream of experience is perceptibly changed by an Odin or a Luther; and if Luther had been a different man, the stream of experience would be different as a result. No one can predict when, or whether, the Hero will step forth.

If history does move in cycles that are neither regular, predictable, nor automatic, what is the nature of that movement? Carlyle's answer is that in the long run life becomes better, both physically and morally. We recall that theism is a "higher level" of worship than pantheism in *Heroes and Hero-Worship*. Individuals make progress, too: "Any opinion he (a man) may form will only serve him for a time, it expands itself daily, for progression is the law of every man: if he be a fool even, still, he must have some power of progress."[9] And history tells us that societies progress: "The progress of man towards higher and nobler developments of whatever is highest and noblest in him, lies not only prophesied to Faith, but now written to the eye of Observation, so that he who runs may read."[10]

Unlike the more optimistic believers in the progress of the species, Carlyle had doubts about his own age. Things move on toward one's own period, and then the rotten and diseased parts of the body politic begin to overwhelm it so progress seems to have ended with one's own time as decay takes over. In *Lectures on the History of Literature* (1838) the eighteenth century was not an era of improvement but of decline; and the signs of a better era are faint. Carlyle hoped in 1838 that Goethe might have a band of disciples to carry on the literary priesthood; but the hope was almost equivalent to blind faith, for no new priest had yet appeared. In other writings of a fairly early date, especially "Characteristics" (1831), Carlyle reconciled the problem of what appeared to be past progress and present standstill.

> The Old has passed away: but, alas, the New appears not in its stead; the Time is still in pangs of travail with

the New. Man has walked in the light of conflagra-
tions, and amid the sound of falling cities; and now
there is darkness, and long watching till it be morning.
. . . Morning also will not fail. Nay, already, as we look
round, streaks of a dayspring are in the east; it is
dawning; when the time shall be fulfilled, it will be
day.[11]

The French Revolution and the death of skepticism
marked the end of one era; and the new period is just on
the horizon. Carlyle's early optimism turned more and
more to denunciation of the present and a wish to turn
back the clock to better times: *Past and Present* glorifies
the Middle Ages, although Carlyle's divided allegiance is
evident.

To the questions of why there is progress, what
qualities in existence make for continual improvement,
answers are given in what Carlyle implies about human
nature and life in general. Like the late nineteenth-
century evolutionists, he has a conviction that progress is
intimately connected with the aggressiveness of the
species itself. He is forever emphasizing the active
principle in man, for men must make, not simply accept,
the world around them. Creation is an unfinished
process in which men participate. This aggressiveness,
this will to work, to mold, to move is what marks us as
human. It provides grounds for believing that the future
will be better than the present. Carlyle asserts that man
has conquered much of the world so far and that he can,
indeed must, continue to mold his environment. He has
a paean to man in *Past and Present* that is Whitmanesque
in its apotheosis of the aggressiveness of human nature:

Difficult? Yes, it will be difficult. The short-fiber cotton;
that too was difficult. The waste cotton-shrub, long
useless, disobedient, as the thistle by the wayside—
have ye not conquered it: made it into beautiful
bandana webs; white woven shirts for men; bright
tinted air-garments wherein flit goddesses? Ye have
shivered mountains asunder, made the hard iron

pliant to you as soft putty: the Forest-giants, Marsh-
Jötuns bear sheaves of golden-grain; Ægir the Sea-
demon himself stretches his back for a sleek highway
to you, and on Firehorses and Windhorses you career.
Ye are most strong. . . . You must try this thing (saving
society). Once try it with the understanding that it will
and shall have to be done. . . . I will bet on you once
more, against all Jötuns; Tailor-gods, Double-barrelled
Law-wards, and Denizens of Chaos whatsoever![12]

Besides human qualities that provide a basis for a belief
in improvement, Carlyle can point to qualities in existence in general. We have already seen how the "light
gleam" draws the imagination on to make a resolution.
Even abyss and uncertainty in life cause us to move
forward. We attempt to solve the mystery and to follow
the gleam.

> A region of Doubt, therefore, hovers forever in the
> background; in Action alone can we have certainty.
> Nay, properly Doubt is the indispensable inexhaust-
> ible material whereon Action works, which Action has
> to fashion into Certainty and Reality; only on a canvas
> of Darkness, such is man's way of being, could the
> many-coloured picture of our Life paint itself and
> shine.[13]

Darkness, doubt, and even danger have an attraction for
us because they call forth a search for the wisdom and
light within the darkness. Progress has its foundation in
the attractive and unfinished qualities of the universe
and in the part of human nature that is ever seeking to
grow, to understand, to expand.

Carlyle identifies progress with increasing complexity
and differentiation. Nature is like a memory bank that
records all the impressions and never forgets. "Every
single event is the offspring not of one, but of all other
events, prior or contemporaneous, and will in its turn
combine with all others to give birth to new."[14] "No
Truth or Goodness realised by man ever dies, or can die;

but is all still here, and, recognised or not, lives and works through endless changes."[15] Because nothing is ever lost from the process, those people in 1830 have a great deal more "history," that is, experience behind them, influencing their responses. We can never turn the clock back and again become pagans like Odin's people because we are building on what has already been apprehended and lived out. Given the assumption that nothing is ever lost, a diagram of history would resemble a funnel. The ancients lived closer to the narrow part than we do; and they led a simpler existence intellectually and physically. The nineteenth century is closer to the larger part of the funnel because there are more events that flow into the modern experience than into the ancient.

The model of the funnel also implies that everything changes qualitatively, and so the Scandinavian perception of truth, for example, cannot be ours. "The angels and demons that can lay prostrate our hearts in the nineteenth century must be of another and more cunning fashion than those that subdued us in the ninth."[16] "No man whatever believes, or can believe, exactly what his grandfather believed . . . he enlarges somewhat, I say; finds somewhat that was credible to his grandfather incredible to him."[17] *Relativity* is the word that describes what Carlyle means, and its connotations, after Einstein, are interesting when seen in connection with a Victorian. Apparently, we do not measure "Truth" by an absolute, unchanging external standard but only by comparing perceptions within the process. We are obliged to use the relationships between things now present in order to make judgments. The funnel is built to expand infinitely, and so we have no "Absolute" by which to judge.

Carlyle's writing suggests this kind of perception. He is certain that the universe is in continual expansion and complexification. Igdrasil has a main trunk that extends in ever new and more delicate branches as one moves farther from the center and toward the present. While

Carlyle speaks of the "Absolute" that draws us on, he also stresses the mystery of the universe of which we know very little. We have only relative grasps of the "Truth." In arguing that Dante's writings are, at the same time, both perennial and outdated, Carlyle writes:

> Any theory of Nature is, at most, temporary; but, on the other hand, all theories contain something within them which is perennial. In Dante that was belief, the communion which the heart of hearts can hold with Nature. The human soul, in fact, develops itself into all sorts of opinions, doctrines which go on nearer and nearer to the truth. All theories approximate more or less to the great Theory, *which remains itself always unknown* (italics mine) and in that proportion contain something which must live. . . . Every philosophy that exists is destined to be embraced, melted down as it were, into some larger philosophy, which, too, will have to suffer the same some day.[18]

Relativity, approximation, continual change are part of Carlyle's intellectual framework, at least in his early writings. The theory makes an impression by its absence and unfinished quality, not by its presence and fullness.

God, in the traditional sense, is absent in this universe in a peculiar way, because the absence is the promise that He is there. The Deity has disappeared, yet we are to act as though He were still present. "Truly it may be said, the Divinity has withdrawn from the Earth; or veils himself in that wide-wasting Whirlwind of a departing Era, wherein the fewest can discern his goings."[19] The disappearance of God and the general unhealthiness and darkness of the times are to be dealt with in a practical manner because periods of unbelief are a natural occurrence—"so that reasonable men deal with it, as the Londoners do with their fogs—go cautiously out into the groping crowd, and patiently carry lanterns at noon; knowing, by a well-grounded faith, that the sun is still in existence, and will one day reappear."[20] One should act as though the "celestial guiding stars" are there; and if one works faithfully in the twilight, the universe will again become intelligible and light.

The infinitude of existence brings out another distinctive facet of Carlyle's thinking: he had no concept of an end in history. Several critics have commented on this point, although they do not elaborate. According to Wellek, Carlyle never thought of a detailed prediction of the future, and he had no concept of the aim of history.[21] Bentley writes: "Carlyle and Nietzsche envisaged a world-process that had no goal and was not wholly determined."[22] These are fair judgments but they invite inquiry into why Carlyle paid little attention to the idea of an end.

Carlyle avoided discussing the traditional kingdom of God at the end of history, a kingdom presumably brought about by the divine initiative. He apparently did so because these traditional notions tend, at their worst, toward fatalism and laissez-faire. If God has all of existence in his hand, the conclusion would logically be that man does not have anything important to do. This passivity conflicts with the structure of Carlyle's thinking. The mystery of the universe, he believes, should cause us to work not to speculate, because no man can know "the times and the seasons." One should not concern himself with the hereafter but with the now, not with heaven but with earth. "Here on Earth we are Soldiers, fighting in a foreign land; that understand not the plan of the campaign, and have no need to understand it; seeing well what is at our hand to be done."[23] It is useless to question, useful *to do*; the end of a man is an action, not a thought.

There is another reason Carlyle virtually omits the kingdom of heaven from his writings. It is related to God's absence as a spur to activity. By the nineteenth century the universe was no longer perceived as existing in three layers, as it had been in the sixteenth century, with everything of value organized in a descending order. In this static view the universe was vertical in the sense that everything good was literally at or near the top. God and heaven were identified with the highest layer. Below it lay earth, with less importance and goodness than heaven, and at the bottom layer of existence was hell.

Heaven, earth, and *hell* are words that Carlyle used but with changed meanings. They all became metaphorical ways to describe earthly existence alone. They referred only to the present existence. The three-layered world had been fused into a single world: heaven was a garden; hell was chaos and disorder. Whatever happened to a man, for good or ill, must happen here on earth. The idea of personal immortality, with its heavenly rewards, is difficult to find in Carlyle's writing. He seems to have a Stoic concept of existence. A person disintegrates at death, with his elements returning to the eternal process of nature. Thus, one finds his fulfillment on earth, or nowhere. It is possible that the increasing inquiry into ideas of social, cultural, and biological evolutionary processes is what made the traditional heaven, earth, and hell less credible to the nineteenth century.

Carlyle's thinking was infused with the notion of process. The ultimate values were not "up" in heaven; they were ahead, in the future. This thought is another link with the absence of God. From the process cosmology comes the focus on a "one-layered" world organized not vertically but horizontally because the process is teleological, oriented toward fulfilling a goal "just beyond" the present. The present is continually seeking to move beyond itself, to become what it is not yet but can become. The present is also a ramification, literally a branching off, from the past. This binding together of past, present, and future in the tree of life, putting the focus on the "just beyond," means that the future grows out of the present and is a fulfillment of the now. This concept of time is a possible explanation for Carlyle's secularism. His kingdom of God is shaped like, grows out of, and is a fulfillment of earthly concerns.

He tells us in *Past and Present* that he can no longer give allegiance to a church and a religion that is otherworldly instead of this-worldly:

> To the core of our heart we feel that this divine thing, which you call Mother Church, does fill the whole world hitherto known, and is and shall be all our salvation and all our desire. And yet—and yet— Behold, though it is an unspoken secret, the world is *wider* than any of us think, Right Reverend! Behold, there are yet other immeasurable Sacrednesses in this that you call Heathenism, Secularity! On the whole, I, in an obscure but most rooted manner, feel that I cannot comply with you. . . . I am, so to speak, in the family-way; with child, of I know not what,— certainly of something far different from this! I have— *Per os Dei*, I have Manchester Cotton-trades, Brom- wicham Iron-trades, American Commonwealths, In- dian Empires, Steam Mechanisms, and Shakespeare Dramas, in my belly; and cannot do it (worship the church as the Tibetans worship the Dali Lama), Right Reverend![24]

The sacred and the secular have become fused; the church must have a social gospel or it will die out—it will no longer have a legitimate function; nor will it be able to provide a credible source of authority and direction. Carlyle is not sure exactly what is being born in his time; but he is certain it must divinize the secular or secularize the sacred.

The second section of this chapter concerns social theory. What kind of society does Carlyle portray as a just one, a garden on earth? To begin with the negative, the new society would not be "Mechanical" because men would realize their mastery over the machines that they had created. To Carlyle a mechanical society means one in which an all-pervading sense of man's helplessness prevails in the face of technology. In "Signs of the Times" he traces the areas that mechanism has taken over. In philosophy, the empiricists have overcome the meta-physicians, and they inquire not about God, man, necessity, and free will but about how ideas are associated in the mind. "One of their philosophers has lately discovered, that 'as the liver secretes bile, so does the brain secrete thought.' "[25] "We are no longer instinctively driven to apprehend, and lay to heart, what is Good and Lovely, but rather to inquire, as onlookers, how it is produced, whence it comes, whither it goes."[26] The empirical mind is detached from its inquiries as part of its method. Then, too, it is investigating something eminently uninteresting, as far as Carlyle is concerned, and so it is naturally detached from its labor.

Religion has also suffered from the encroachments of scientific attitudes because it has come to be a vast system of calculating rewards and punishments, "a matter, as all others now are, of Expediency and Utility; whereby some smaller quantum of earthly enjoyment may be ex-changed for a far larger quantum of celestial enjoyment. Thus Religion too is a Profit, a working for wages."[27] Even "Truth" has been changed from something mys-terious, holy, and compelling, something for which a man could die, to mere accuracy or probability. The soul has gone out of religion, philosophy, literature, and all the areas in which man expressed himself creatively.

"Signs of the Times" was written to impress upon the reader man's ability to transcend the mechanism of the age. The message is that man made the chains; he can also break them asunder—spirit over matter. In a later writing, *Latter-Day Pamphlets* (1850), Carlyle denounces England's actual operating principles with the "Pig Philosophy." A few of the tenets reveal his dislikes:

> "Define the Whole Duty of Pigs." It is the mission of universal Pighood, and the duty of all Pigs, at all times, to diminish the quantity of unattainable and increase that of attainable. All knowledge and device and effort

ought to be directed thither and thither only; Pig Science, Pig Enthusiasm and Devotion have this one aim. It is the Whole Duty of Pigs.

"Have you Law and Justice in Pigdom?" Pigs of observation have discerned that there is, or was once supposed to be, a thing called justice.

"Where do they find that (lawyers are oracles of God) written?" In Coke upon Lyttelton.

"Who made Coke?" Unknown: the maker of Coke's wig is discoverable.[28]

Carlyle seemed to think life had become a caricature, that humans had been reduced to animals, that philosophy was based on the pleasure principle, and that these tendencies, part and parcel of mechanism, needed to be reversed.

Carlyle's most extensive discussion of how the world could be reformed is found in Books 3 and 4 of *Past and Present*. One of the first things he would do is eliminate the huge gap between the rich and the working poor. The present aristocrats, who receive special privileges because of inherited wealth and noble birth, must be replaced by superior men who merit the title of *aristos*, "best." The "best men" will have the wisdom to govern the classes under them in such a way that the interests of England and of each class will be served in the long run. The present aristocracy is almost totally useless because they do no work but do collect rents and shoot partridges. They are parasites on the body politic; and, if necessary, they should be overthrown by force. When the "best men" are discovered, the old nobility should be thrown out of power: "For if you do mean to obey God-made superiors, your first step is to sweep out the Tailor-made ones; order them, under penalties, to vanish, to make ready for vanishing!"[29] Carlyle's sympathy for the Chartist movement also reflects his belief that power must be used in a judicious manner to dislodge the present governing classes. But it should be noted that

"Chartism" (1839) and *Past and Present* (1843) are not products of the reactionary Carlyle of a few years later. He believes in 1839 that the workers have the potential of making the government redress some of the wrongs they suffer.

Carlyle's belief that England's salvation lay in the middle-class "captains of industry" and their rechanneling the energy of the proletariat marks him as a radical of the times, although he was not aligned politically with any of the parties, neither Whig nor Tory nor Radical. He sounds Marxian in his call to the masses to regenerate England:

> Awake, ye noble Workers. . . . Let God's justice, let pity, nobleness and manly valour, with more gold-purses or with fewer, testify themselves in this your brief Life-transit to all the Eternities, the Gods and Silences. It is to you I call; for ye are not dead, ye are already half-alive: there is in you a sleepless dauntless energy, the prime-matter of all nobleness in man. Honour to you in your kind. It is to you I call: ye know at least this, That the mandate of God to His creature man is: Work![30]

The proletariat represents a vast reservoir of nobility and energy for both Marx and Carlyle. However, theoretically, Marx would have the proletariat rule in his new society, whereas Carlyle would have the workers governed by the captains of industry, who stand halfway between the wealthy owners and the workers.

Throwing out the present aristocracy and properly directing the energy of the masses is only a vague first step in the building of a new society. The relationship between classes must be fundamentally changed. The worker's human dignity should be restored to him in various ways. To begin with he must be paid "a fair day's wages for a fair day's work," so that he knows he can provide food, shelter, and clothes for himself and his family. He should get work, not welfare doles. Carlyle also favors a universal education law, so that the workers have the information necessary to participate in their society.

> That thought, reflection, articulate utterance and un-
> derstanding be awakened in these individual million
> heads, which are the atoms of your Chaos: there is no
> other way of illuminating any Chaos! The sum-total of
> intelligence that is found in it, determines the extent of
> order that is possible for your Chaos.[31]

The workers are to be educated so that they will make rational demands of their superiors and will accept reasonable measures proposed by the governors. The education can be the groundwork for a shared under-standing of the needs of the English nation and of all classes; it supplies an element of social cohesion. Carlyle advocates passage by the legislature of an education bill with the establishment of an education service and secretary of the department to carry out the designs of the bill.[32]

The fair wages and education give the worker dignity and a chance to participate in the goals of the society, but other reforms are also needed. The whole value system must be reconstituted. "To be a noble Master, among noble Workers, will again be the first ambition with some few; to be a rich Master only the second."[33] Wealth is a less important goal than nobility, which Carlyle defines as the earned respect of one's fellow man. And, of course, the workers can be noble, too. In effect, Carlyle wants to replace one religion with another—the new one having "manly valour" instead of "Mammon" as its ideal.

Carlyle is at his most radical, and most constructive, when he advocates joint ownership of the means of production. He asks in "Chartism": "Can the labourer, by thrift and industry, hope to rise to mastership; or is such hope cut off from him? How is he related to his employer; by bonds of friendliness and mutual help; or by hostility, opposition, and chains of mutual necessity alone?"[34] And in *Past and Present* Carlyle cautiously suggests that the worker should become part owner of the enterprise:

> A question arises here: whether in some ulterior, perhaps some not far-distant stage of this "Chivalry of Labour," your Master-Worker may not find it possible, and needful, to grant his Workers permanent *interest* in his enterprise and theirs? So that it become, in practical result, what in essential fact and justice it ever is, a joint enterprise; all men, from the Chief Master down to the lowest Overseer and Operative, economically as well as loyally concerned for it?[35]

In suggesting that the worker be given permanent interest, that is, part ownership of the business, both Carlyle and Marx are using an essentially conservative opinion with a radical interpretation. Edmund Burke, the conservative of nearly a century earlier, was of the opinion that only property (land) owners had a real interest in the fortunes of the government. Carlyle and Marx agree with Burke in principle; but they want to spread the property to the greater part of the population. If everyone owned a part of his business, he would have a stake in how well the enterprise went. Carlyle assumes that the worker would then not only be industrious but also loyal and happy because he has the pride of owning and directing. However, Carlyle would not allow his proletariat any great power in the company's board of directors or in the nation's government; the workers are to obey their superiors when the leaders satisfy their needs. Marx would have the proletariat govern everything because there would be no distinction between owner and worker in the classless society.

Although joint ownership of the means of production probably was to his Victorian readers the most shocking proposal Carlyle made, it was only one of the radical measures he proposed to improve the lot of the work-ingman. These measures have as their premise more governmental control and a reversal of the principle of laissez-faire.

> He ("the present editor") knows not, it is for others than he to know, in what specific ways it may be feasible to interfere, with Legislation, between the Workers and the Master-Workers;—knows only and sees, what all men are beginning to see, that Legislative interference, and interferences not a few are indispensable; that as lawless anarchy of supply-and-demand, on market-wages alone, this province of things cannot longer be left.[36]

More governmental control of business in the interests of labor, Carlyle felt, would be a positive step toward liberating the worker from the ups and downs of the market. Once he had contracts and laws in his favor, the laborer would have some security about what his wages would be, whether or not he actually had the job, for how long, under what conditions he could be dismissed, and so forth.

The legislative control of business would also insure the enforcement of proper sanitary regulations, pollution checks, and the provision of recreation parks in the factory town.

> The Legislature, even as it now is, could order all dingy Manufacturing Towns to cease from their soot and darkness; to let-in the blessed sunlight, the blue of Heaven, and become clear and clean; to burn their coal-smoke, namely, and make flame of it. Baths, free air, a wholesome temperature, ceilings twenty feet high, might be ordained, by Act of Parliament, in all establishments licensed as Mills.
>
> Every toiling Manchester, its smoke and soot all burnt, ought it not, among so many world-wide conquests, to have a hundred acres or so of free greenfield, with trees on it, conquered, for its little children to disport in; for its all-conquering workers to take a breath of twilight air in?[37]

Considering the environment as it is at present, it is interesting to speculate what might have happened had Carlyle's suggestions of 1843 been adopted immediately. Carlyle was ahead of his time—and ours—in perceiving that human values, like health and happiness, have higher priority than businesses, prosperity, and the profit motive. He felt that British industry was strong enough to survive a few regulations cutting down its power. When the rights of "these rickety perishing souls of infants" confronted the interests of the cotton trade in world markets, the cotton trade could take its chances.[38]

The last of Carlyle's proposals from *Past and Present* concerning social reconstruction was an emigration act. For every worker who could not find a job in England, the government should provide the opportunity to settle in an underdeveloped part of the Commonwealth, or even where there were no other Englishmen. In the long run this emigration act would help the economy because the Englishmen who settled in faraway places would be predisposed to trade with the mother country.[39] Emigration would also lower the labor supply and push wages up to a decent level for those who stayed behind. Besides the economic facts, resettlement was an exciting challenge for those who were going to wilderness areas, with the opportunity to claim land for their own in fresh territory. Carlyle speaks enthusiastically of America, which offered vast areas of undeveloped land, free for the claiming, along with close ties to the settlers' own country, England.

In spite of the progressive nature of these suggestions for social reform, Carlyle nevertheless envisioned a hierarchical society based on respect for the designated leaders. Book 2 of *Past and Present* is devoted to a colorful description of a medieval monastery whose affairs, financial and spiritual, were in shambles until Abbot Samson was elected director. Samson was a man of honesty, courage, wisdom, and decisive action; he set the affairs in order and commanded the respect of the other monks. The social system worked so well because he was a man of merit, and his associates recognized it and obeyed. He had something indispensable to give them, a source of authority; and they had something indispensable for him, service. The same principle held true in the world outside the monastery, where the serfs exchanged crops for the military protection of the lord. Social relations were non-exploitive because each part of society needed the other. The key to the stability was loyalty and obedience on the part of the lower classes to those above them.

The healthy society, then, is based on worship of a good Great Man, who sails by the "eternal lode-stars." The Hero is the emblem of a whole people's character, and if they are righteous, their choice of a leader will be just. "What man dost thou honour? Which is thy ideal of a man; or nearest that?" is the most important question that can be asked.[40] Hero worship "is the soul of all social business among men; . . . the doing of it well, or the doing of it ill, measures accurately what degree of well-being or of ill-being there is in the world's affairs."[41] The best society is a hierarchical one based on a just despotism instead of atomistic individualism. Carlyle wants a truly collective society where competition and profits cannot go unchecked, and where each class plays a limited, but indispensable, role.

The Middle Ages in some sense provides a model by which to reconstruct nineteenth-century England. Although Carlyle is drawn to the past, he recognizes that the future cannot be modeled on a society that existed 800 years earlier. Too much has happened in the world, with the advent of capitalism, world trade, and industrialization, for England to become what it was in medieval days. However, the principle of a hierarchical society is a good one, according to Carlyle. The practical workings of the hierarchy have become disorderly, though, and the answer is to make the system work effectively under present conditions. Between the Middle Ages and modern times the bond between the top and bottom of the system has eroded because neither class can now fulfill its part of the unwritten contract. An aristocracy that once had provided a necessary service in exchange for necessary goods now was functionless, since the modern state supplied military protection. Now the top of the hierarchy was contributing nothing, yet it maintained the privileges it once had. It fenced off land, governed the country in a slipshod manner, and shot game birds in its spare time. The lower classes, which once had been agrarian, had to turn to the factory for jobs and there were not enough jobs to meet the demand. The bottom of the hierarchy, through no fault of its own, had lost its indispensability and consequent bargaining position. With an abundant labor supply at its disposal, the real centers of power—the wealthy industrialists—felt no responsibility to the workers, since the latter were easily replaceable. In Carlyle's language, Parliament, made up of aristocrats, could not care less about the plight of the workers: Rigmarole and Dolittle were always busy with "their own clique, and self-conceited crotchets."[42] Carlyle clearly saw that the workers needed some bargaining power, for the proposals that would lower the labor supply, push wages up, and perhaps eventually give the worker part ownership of the business would strengthen the ties between classes and would weaken the power of the owners. If the workers were once again a necessary part of the whole system, social stability and healthiness would be the result.

For someone who labeled economics the "Dismal Science" and who urged a renewal of the "inner man," not the social environment, Carlyle's legislative proposals in "Signs of the Times," show a keen grasp of a practical socialistic economic theory. They incorporate his faith in human action and his belief that religion and a just society must go hand in hand. Frederick William Roe, whose book on *The Social Philosophy of Carlyle and Ruskin* is one of the basic studies in this area, summarizes four points that Carlyle's theories heralded: the preservation of human dignity in industry; more collective control and ownership; increased partnership of labor with capital; and work as an expression of the creative impulse.[43] All these results would come about after the fundamental changes in attitudes and institutions were made—changes that would give all classes common interests and ideals.

Past and Present ends with a grand vision of the earth made into the Garden of Eden by the work of men's hands. It is the most stirring and most optimistic view of a reformed society that appears in Carlyle's writings.

> Some "Chivalry of Labour," some noble Humanity and practical Divineness of Labour, will yet be realised on this Earth. Or why *will*; why do we pray to Heaven, without setting our own shoulder to the wheel? The Present, if it will have the Future accomplish, shall itself commence. Thou who prophesiest, who believest, begin thou to fulfill. Here or nowhere, now equally as at any time!
>
> But it is to you, ye Workers, who do already work, and are as grown men, noble and honourable in a sort, that the whole world calls for new work and nobleness. Subdue mutiny, discord, wide-spread despair, by manfulness, justice, mercy and wisdom. Chaos is dark, deep as Hell; let light be, and there is instead a green flowery World. . . . Sooty Hell of mutiny and savagery and despair can, by man's energy, be made a kind of Heaven; cleared of its soot, of its mutiny, of its need to mutiny; the everlasting arch of Heaven's azure overspanning *it* too, and its cunning mechanisms and tall chimney-steeples, as a birth of Heaven; God and all men looking on it well pleased. . . .
>
> Noble fruitful Labour, growing ever nobler, will come forth,—the grand sole miracle of Man; whereby Man has risen from the low places of this Earth, very literally, into divine Heavens. Ploughers, Spinners, Builders; Prophets, Poets, Kings; Brindleys and Goethes, Odins and Arkwrights; all martyrs, and noble men, and gods are of one grand Host; im-

measurable; marching ever forward since the begin-
nings of the World.[44]

One of the most intriguing aspects of this vision of a New
World is its apotheosis of man. Prometheus is "marching
to Zion"; Carlyle has blended the Aeschylean belief that
man will transcend his limitations with the Hebrew stress
on social justice. Through work, making, molding his
surroundings, man rises from the low places into the
high ones: nothing can stop him if he has the will to
conquer, for he has gone forward in the past and he will
make progress in the future. Men and the gods participate in the remaking of the earth; they are all "one grand
Host." The working classes, the ploughers, prophets,
and Arkwrights, have been divinized, for their work has
been made into the work of the heavenly kingdom.
Carlyle's catalog of the true nobility of the times, the
workers, calls to mind Walt Whitman's divinization of
man or Carl Sandburg's songs about the city of
Chicago—all three of these writers praise man's energy
and his instinctive expression of himself in the creation of
his world. The epic is written by men who have become
heroic through the use of their wits, strength, and their
tools.

Returning to Carlyle's attitude toward work, with its
stress on human activity in relation to God's will, we
remember that the force was supplied by men. They
either wove the garments so that the immanent deity
could be seen, or they built the wall in accordance with
the specifications of a remote, transcendent God. One
sees the same stress on human energy and purposefulness in the vision of *Past and Present:* "Sooty Hell . . . can,
by man's energy, be made a kind of Heaven." The
emphasis is on the heroic power of the common worker;
he is great and noble; he will overcome the limitations
that his surroundings impose.

Besides the focus on man and his tools in Carlyle's epic
vision, the present time is also emphasized. The nostal-

gia for medieval life has been replaced by technology, the modern period, and human inventiveness.

A recognition of the dual nature of time, with its promise and its threat, appears often in Carlyle's writings, but no matter which pole is emphasized, the call is always for men to put their shoulder to the wheel. His essays on Ireland in 1848 state that "now it (the Irish problem) has all come down upon us; and we welter among it, on the edge of huge perils: and we must alter it, or prepare to perish. Surely, if ever for any country in the world, remedial measures are needed for Ireland now!"[45] The threat of the present should, and indeed must, act as a spur to decisive action. England, and perhaps the world, is on the brink; and she must choose this day whom she will serve and where she will go. Time, in these and later essays, does not go slowly and regularly. It erupts into consciousness and demands that action be taken. The metaphor of the present that Carlyle uses in 1867 is Niagara Falls, whose mad rush will not wait for careful meditation on the possibilities, or for Rigmarole to propose a Parliamentary bill.

The promise of the present time is especially evident in *Past and Present* and in early essays like "Signs of the Times" and *Sartor Resartus*. In the latter book he uses Goethe's phrase "time is my seed-field" to express the idea that when we work, we body forth the heavenly eternal in the time-space world. The present is full of opportunity for service and satisfaction.[46] In "Signs of the Times" Carlyle argues that no limitations, whether they be of a fatalistic philosophy, or an age of mechanism, or the finitude of earth and time, can stop us if we are alert and doing the work we can clearly see.

The present moment contains yet another potential, related to that of the seed field, for it gives us the opportunity to plant our personality in the whole character of existence. The present moment "is thus an infinite arena, where infinite interests are played out; not an action of man but will have its truth realised and will go on for ever. His most insignificant action, for some are more so than others, carries its print of this endless duration."[47] The moments are emptily running by us until we choose to do this or that, and so express our purposes within time; and by our doing something, we change the nature of the time stream. Man is involved as a participant, not as a detached observer of the process. The present moment is heavy with significance only when we act; otherwise it goes by without our mark; and it will eventually extinguish us. We decide whether we make any difference in the world or not.

The apotheosis of man and the accent on the present moment are complementary to another thrust of the quotation, the secularization of the kingdom of heaven. Carlyle had seen that industrialization could not be escaped and that society could not retreat into the Middle Ages. Instead, the industrial system must be understood and controlled, so that its effects could be transformed from something which destroyed human dignity to something that could be used to enhance life. The earth, with its machines and factories, is the primary reality; and what we do or do not make of it decides the future. In Book 4 of *Past and Present* the sacred and the secular are no longer antithetical "spheres," they have been united.

The ringing phrases and the accompanying optimism of *Past and Present* were replaced only five years later with much sterner measures for social reform and gloomy predictions that nothing would really work. One of the most noticeable differences in Carlyle's writings of the earlier and later periods is that his faith in the common man has turned to fear. *Sartor Resartus* (1833) announced confidently that all men were emblems of the godlike; *Heroes and Hero-Worship* (1841) suggested that anyone could become heroic, either by being or by recognizing a Great Man; *Past and Present* (1843) cautiously implied that the worker should share in the ownership and control of the business that employs him. The underlying assumption is that the common man has the intelligence to decide what is in his best interests in the long run. In Book 4 of *Past and Present* the worker has become the backbone of the new society, for he provides its energy and literally makes its mechanisms work. He is the divinized source for spiritual regeneration, too, because he has a soul in him. Carlyle's later writings, however, show a repudiation of democratic principles: the Irish essays (1848), *Latter-Day Pamphlets* (1850), "The Nigger Question" (1849), and "Shooting Niagara: And After?" (1867). The common man, who once was a reservoir of regenerating forces, has become identified with undisciplined, passionate, and mindless instincts. The wise are few; the foolish are many. Even the captains of industry from *Past and Present* must use stern measures because the masses they command can only understand the most simple, immediate reward and punishment. They cannot comprehend long-range goals because they are childish. The captain addresses his troops thus:

> To each of you I will then say: Here is work for you; strike into it with manlike, soldierlike obedience and heartiness, according to the methods here prescribed,—wages follow for you without difficulty; all manner of just remuneration, and at length emancipation itself follows. Refuse to strike into it; shirk the heavy labour, disobey the rules,—I will admonish and endeavour to incite you; if in vain, I will flog you; if still in vain, I will at last shoot you,—and make God's Earth, and the forlorn-hope in God's Battle, free of you.[48]

Given this twist to Carlyle's view of the common man, it is small wonder that he believes democracy will not work. The masses have little reason and much undisciplined instinct, and they can be swayed by any promises the demagogue makes. Therefore, the answer to what governmental reforms are needed cannot be democracy but oligarchy (rule by only the best, which are few).

> Many men vote; but in the end, you will infallibly find, none counts except the few who were *in the right*. Unit

of that class (the "right") against as many zeros (masses' votes) as you like! If the King's thought *is* according to the will of God, or to the law appointed for this Universe, I can assure your Lordship the King will ultimately carry that, were he but one in it against the whole world.[49]

The best social system, according to the Carlyle of the 1850s and 1860s, is minority rule by the elect, or those reasonable people who can read the laws of the universe.

What had been a hierarchy in *Past and Present* with each segment being necessary to the other's existence, and hence, with a certain reciprocity and bargaining power for each class, has in *Latter-Day Pamphlets* become a rigid system in which the lower classes are actually a burden. A military regime has become Carlyle's favorite model for reorganizing society. In the army, the lower ranks are obedient, loyal, and respectful to the upper ranks. There is stability in this social system; and law and order, even at the expense of crushing dissent, is the paramount goal.

The "open universe" of the early Carlyle, where ideas freely compete, is gone. It has been replaced by a highly structured world where sin is sin, evil is evil; and only the elect can tell the difference between the two. In the "open universe" that was continually complexifying, growing, and absorbing diverse experiences, each man's life and acts made a difference. Truth never was, it always was to come; and no one could see the end of the process. In *Latter-Day Pamphlets*, "Truth" is identified with the will of the elite, who alone have knowledge of what Carlyle called the laws of the universe. Change, flux, and becoming in the early Carlyle have been replaced by rigidity, stasis, and "eternal truths." What was once unpredictable and elusive has now settled into rigid dichotomies, with the elect acting in God's name and functioning as his representatives on earth.

Furthermore, the later Carlyle has decided that the common man is simply a childish creature who needs only sensual pleasures to keep him happy. Keep the masses quiet with bread and work; and that is all the situation requires. They can be manipulated and controlled because they are subject to easily satisfiable needs, so rewards and punishments work well. The germs of an Animal Farm or a Brave New World are here in the late Carlyle.

Most of Carlyle's writings before 1848 can be labeled progressive, while the ones after that are embittered. What happened to change his view of the common man, from someone godlike to someone animal-like? What made him want a military regime for a government rather than a cooperative democratic system? Why did he view the environment as filthy, poisonous, and evil in his later writings?

Certainly the European revolutions of 1848 and the reaction to them must have affected his views. In England, social unrest and the Irish problem made the country's political future uncertain and gave rise to a call for radical and urgent solutions. Besides these external social conditions, there are events in Carlyle's personal life that may have contributed to his feelings of desperation and crisis. His stormy marriage with Jane Welsh was nearly dissolved in the years between 1846 and 1847.[50] Jane, probably without sufficient justification, suspected him of too intimate a friendship with Lady Ashburton. The jealousy and ill-will generated over the Ashburtons was one more flaw in a marriage that was continually plagued with sharp words and empty promises that things would one day be better. Although Jane remained with Carlyle, the scars were always present.

For two years, around 1848 and 1849, Carlyle seemed to be in a severe emotional depression that looked as though it would never end. He wrote in his journal:

> How lonely I am now grown in the world; how hard, many times as if I were made of stone! All the old tremulous affection lies in me, but it is as if frozen. So mocked, and scourged, and driven mad by contradictions, it has, as it were, lain down in a kind of iron sleep.[51]

The severe depression could have come from a combina-
tion of marital problems and the realization that he was
now middle-aged. His mother, perhaps his closest
confidant, died in 1853. With her death, he became the
oldest generation. His father had died long before, in
1832. Carlyle had spent most of his life hoping for a
"better tomorrow." He was never satisfied with himself,
his writings, or anything around him; and he had always
comforted himself with a vague hope of future improvement. In 1848 he was fifty-three years old and beginning
to realize that the best was already past instead of in the
future. His personal problems, coupled with revolutionary events in Europe in 1848, were perhaps enough
to alter his views of the character of existence and the
possibility of being happy.

In conclusion, whether one is reading Carlyle up to
1848 or after that date, human activity and the secular
world loom large in the vast scope of the universe. In the
early Carlyle, man is necessary to the ongoing process of
history because his acts affect the nature of the outcome.
The universe is an ever-complexifying one in which
every personality leaves its imprint on the future. And
man matters because he is an active being, who is always
"on the way" to fulfilling some purpose, always seeking
to understand, to resolve, and to grow. Every time he
finds an answer or accomplishes a task, he has the
possibility of moving closer to the "great Theory," which
always remains unknown. The truth is a-making, not
already made; and hence man participates in the process
of history in an important way. Instead of the traditional
notion that God is both alpha and omega, and He makes
the end a recapitulation of the beginning, Carlyle, in
keeping with evolutionary concepts, has muted the
emphasis on the end by suggesting that it will never
come, or at least that we must act as if it will never come.
And if there is an omega, its character will be different
from the alpha because of the human decisions made
along the way.

In removing the stress on a trans-historical kingdom of heaven that recapitulates paradise, Carlyle has, in large measure, gotten rid of the static notion of existence. Popular Calvinism understood earth and history as only preparation for eternal rewards; the secular derived its significance from what it pointed toward, not for what it was in itself. And history for Calvin and the tradition ran according to a predetermined plan, never changing in essence from beginning to end, and, ultimately, never being affected by human acts. All things were in the Almighty's hand and He held the initiative. The proper human response was to trust God and surrender oneself to his mercy.

In the nineteenth century it was difficult to believe in "essences" and "eternals" after the scientific findings of Darwin, and the many books that traced the long development of the world. Process and change came to be part of the metaphysics of the age, and Carlyle was not unaware of the different world view that these concepts necessitated. One could hardly accept the idea of fundamental, qualitative change in the universe and still believe in predestined plans of creation. And once one was convinced that human acts left their mark on the stream of experience, he could hardly think that God alone took all the initiatives. Instead, Carlyle is saying that any progress in history rests in large measure on how men accept responsibility for what they do. The good man does not live by laissez-faire and does not wait for preexistent laws to work themselves out; he puts his shoulder to the wheel in the belief that if he does not, the desired outcome will never come about. He does not wait for help from any quarter; he fights nobly and with determination, knowing that he can and must succeed.

Although the open-ended universe, which has room for real human creativity and initiative, disappears in Carlyle's later writings, the focus remains on man and his world. The God who had been "just ahead" becomes more and more remote; and the accent on process is

replaced by one on moral order. However, the discrep-
ancy between the laws of the universe and those laws
by which society actually runs is so great that immediate
and radical attempts are needed to bring the one in
conformity with the other. The times are teeming with
either destruction or deliverance, Carlyle tells us, and
unless we move to build our society according to the
cosmic pattern of justice, we will perish by our own
indecision. Men play a crucial part in determining
whether England will survive at all, depending upon
how well they meet the challenges that the new age has
brought. They must take the responsibility; no one "up
above" will.

Besides the focus on human initiative and responsibility, Carlyle's writings show an acceptance of the secular,
with all its "soot and mutiny." He does not want to pass
beyond the factory system by returning to the wilderness
or to the Middle Ages; he wants to transform Manchester
and use its energy for purposes that enhance human life.
Heaven is not beyond history; it is in it. Either Manchester is made into a Garden of Eden or it remains an
inferno. But the time is the present; the place is here on
earth; and the principal actor is man.

Conclusion

Thus, we can safely conclude that there is a definite shift in Carlyle's view of the early and late Hero, the Great Man, labor, and of a just society. The early Hero is depicted as a mediator, persuader, and as a sign of the divine in the flesh. The later Hero becomes the Grand Inquisitor who is the righteous judge and executor; he can do no wrong. In the case of either the early or late Great Man, God is absent from the world's stage, and man becomes the principal actor.

In Carlyle's writings before 1848, labor is the artistic creation of man, who supplies the force and even some of the direction; after 1848, labor tends more to be work in accordance with moral order. His vision of a just society in the future is one of harmonious relations between labor and business, fair wages, education, decent housing, health conditions, and so forth.

In discussing the changed Calvinism of Carlyle's writings and times, perhaps we could best focus on four major points: God, man, history, and modernity. The first point includes Carlyle's general attitudes toward religion and theology. Of course, it has often been mentioned, with warrant, that Carlyle was no systematic thinker, much less a systematic theologian. Just the same, his thirty some volumes, written over forty years, reveal something of the general tendencies of the age, and they contain implications for the history of religious thought. Carlyle had much to say about God, man, the nature of existence, that is, about ultimate concerns. Directly or indirectly, his writings reflect an approach toward religious questions that is quite different from traditional Calvinism.

On the other hand, there are in Carlyle's letters some quite orthodox religious pronouncements. Some of Carlyle's personal letters suggest that it could be argued that he was extremely orthodox and traditional in his notions of God. It is true that some of his letters are as conservative as those written by his mother. Concerning immortality, Carlyle once wrote: "Surely, surely there is a Life beyond Death; and that gloomy Portal leads to a purer and an abiding Mansion."[1] On another occasion, the death of his twenty-seven-year-old sister Margaret, Carlyle assures his mother that the whole family will someday be together in paradise.[2] More than once the traditional religious belief that we are all in God's hand appears in Carlyle's letters.[3] However, these conservative sentiments almost always appear in letters written to his mother, who was worried about her son's beliefs and who would have been deeply hurt by any unorthodoxy. In other cases, these traditional sentiments appear in letters consoling family and friends on the death of someone close. The assurances of immortality quoted above were written after the aunt of Jane Welsh Carlyle had died and after Margaret Carlyle had died at an early age. Carlyle would have been unfeeling had he written anything unorthodox at a time when the family wanted comfort.

When Carlyle is not writing to the family, or writing letters of consolation, he sounds much more like the "doubting Thomas." He himself gave up early aspirations of being a clergyman because he could not accept traditional doctrines; and for the same reasons he did not attend church, except on rare occasions.[4] When the popular clergyman, F. D. Maurice, wrote a pamphlet demonstrating that the Thirty-nine Articles were a charter of religious liberty and reasonable belief, Carlyle privately wrote a sarcastic jingle that went:

Thirty-Nine English Articles,
Ye wondrous little particles,
Did God shape His universe really by you?

In that case I swear it,
And solemnly declare it,
This logic of Maurice's is true.[5]

Carlyle liked to think of himself as a man of integrity and independence who would not give allegiance to man-made creeds, Thirty-nine Articles included, which he identified with hypocrisy and sham.

In the letters to colleagues and old school friends, Carlyle is considerably less orthodox than he is in the family correspondence. In a letter to Henry Inglis, he muses: "It is a solitary kind of world; yet it is a world; and I imagine had a Maker."[6] The letter to John Sterling in which Teufelsdröckh denies any personality, name, or attributes to "God" is another example of Carlyle's refusal to accept traditional Christianity. To John Stuart Mill, Carlyle writes:

> All that of Natural Theology, and a Demiourgos sitting *outside* the world, and exhibiting "marks of design" is as deplorable to me as it is to you. Immortality also till of late years I never could so much as see the possibility of; till now in some sense the certainty and philosophic necessity of it became manifest. And so I live in a kind of Christian Islam (which signifies "submission to God"), and say at all turns of Fortune, "God is great" and also "God is good," and know not aught else that I could say.[7]

Carlyle's skepticism, his doubts, and his search for beliefs that were credible and reasonable are all evident in these passages. His "acceptance" of the concept of immortality, for example, is unconvincing—the result of submission to necessity rather than the product of reason.

Describing himself, Carlyle is chary of terms like *conservative* or *traditional*. He enjoyed being considered eccentric, whether in dress or in beliefs. His whole life could be seen as an attempt to define himself as unique: his prose style, philosophy, personal habits, and his outdated overcoats and hats were calculated to show

how distinct he was; and surely "Carlylese" and books like *Sartor Resartus* are products of a unique personality. Carlyle labeled his own thinking "speculative radicalism," dissociating it from any sect or party and also from the practical, political radicals of his day. "In *thought,* I am the deepest Radical alive in this Island, but allow it to rest there, (not getting politically involved) having other to do."[8]

Carlyle, then, was unorthodox in his doubts and questions, according to his own assessment of himself and according to those of many readers, like Sterling. How, more exactly, did the unorthodoxy operate in his thinking? How did it affect his ideas of God, religion, revelation, and free will?

First of all, Carlyle's acknowledged starting point for "God-talk" was different from that of his sixteenth-century predecessors. Revelation of divinity for the orthodox Calvinist came from above, on God's initiative. The primary means of revelation were the Scriptures and the divine Jesus Christ. The revelation was knowledge of the majesty of God, a knowledge that would bring reasoning and debate to an end and cause one to simply trust the grace of the Almighty. The divine initiative was behind the revelation because God chose to reveal himself—no efforts on the part of man could bring knowledge. Carlyle began with the opposite end of the spectrum from the orthodox Calvinist, with human experience. Man's searching, testing mind is what gives him knowledge of the divine; he seeks God, and by his own efforts discovers something that is credible to him. Carlyle's starting point was "the experienced facts of things interpreted by the intelligence of man."[9] In Carlyle's own words: "One has got two eyes to look with; also a mind capable of knowing, of believing: that is all the creed I will at this time insist on."[10]

Not only did Carlyle make human credibility the criterion for truth, but he also widened the traditional channels for knowledge of the divine. Calvin could insist on the Scriptures as revelation; but in the nineteenth century, biblical criticism had removed much of the once-for-all character of the Bible. In commenting on a clergyman's use of a biblical passage to prove a point, Carlyle writes that the minister built a tower on I Corinthians 13 "till it soared far above all human science and experience, and flatly contradicted all that,— founded solely on a little text of *writing* in an ancient Book!" He continues, "Authentic 'writings' of the Most High, were they found in old Books only? They were in the stars and on the rocks, and in the brain and heart of every mortal."[11] One reads nature; he explores the world of science; he examines his own experience to find knowledge of the divine. Revelation does not come down from heaven once and for all, but it is searched for on earth.

Relating Truth to credibility and to historical circumstances, as Carlyle does, means that our concepts of God must change from era to era. An obvious example is that the notion of God's personality has given way to a totally non-anthropomorphic deity. But how do these changes come about? Because man continually searches to find significance in the world and makes attempts to define a small particle in relation to the whole, religious conceptions will inevitably change from age to age.

> The divinities and demons, the witches, spectres and fairies, are vanished from the world, never again to be recalled: but the Imagination, which created these, still lives, and will forever live, in man's soul; and can again pour its wizard light over the Universe, and summon forth enchantments as lovely or impressive, and which its sister faculties will not contradict.[12]

Poetry, work, and religion have a common source in the human imagination, which bodies forth the unseen. Religious conceptions must change from age to age in order to maintain their credibility—man must be able to believe in and act upon his religion. The capacity for changing the present reality structure, or world view, has its source in the fancy.

Carlyle's writings, then, show the conscious recognition that ideas of God and the universe change from age to age. Did he realize how radical the consequences of his own thinking were for the history of religious thought? Carlyle knew he was a "speculative Radical"; but I doubt he ever realized just how far he had gone in remolding our language about God. Besides removing the idea of personality from the divinity, he had also begun to shake the foundations of our notion of God's omnipotence.

The Calvinist conception of God's omnipotence resolves itself into two ideas of God: that He is the cosmic pattern; and that He works in nature, history, and human life. The concept of God that is reflected in Carlyle's writings is different from that of Calvin even though the same two aspects of the divine appear. When Carlyle speaks of the pattern-law aspect, he does so in order to call men to work. God has set up the standard, but we are responsible for living, socially and individually, in accordance with it. He sets up the plumb line; but He will not build the wall—that is our task. When Carlyle speaks of the immanent divinity, the active mover, he is also calling men to work. The divine is gone from the universe until we weave the garments by which He may be seen. Man's activity and his divine characteristics as either master workman or artistic creator occupy Carlyle's attention.

Carlyle's intentions for describing the two aspects of God's nature are opposite from those of Calvin. Calvin asserts that God is literally All; He has the plan for creation and in the last analysis He carries it out. Men's acts cannot change the final outcome. Men are ultimately insignificant before Almighty God, according to Calvin: God holds the crucial initiatives. For Carlyle, man and his acts are of decisive significance; and man can save himself through his work. (In Carlyle's later writings the "can save" becomes the desperate "must save" himself.)

If one claims that men are crucial to the historical process, as Carlyle does, he has shifted the whole spectrum.

What happens to the Calvinist universe in Carlyle's writings is not that either of the two expressions of God's omnipotence is neglected but that they are split apart. In his early career he wrote about immanent power, which is compatible with the kind of humanism found in his writings. In his later career he emphasized the transcendent moral order aspect of God. This, too, is compatible with the belief that man makes his world, for once the standard is set up, man is responsible for himself and his world. The Greeks believed in fate and moral order, yet they were humanistic. Either aspect of God can be reconciled with a humanistic concept of man; but if the two aspects of pattern and mover are kept together, the humanism is gone—man is in the hands of Almighty God. Calvin kept the two notions together; Carlyle could not because his intentions were the opposite of Calvin.

Besides removing personality from God, and eroding the belief in his omnipotence, Carlyle's writings also contain some implications for the idea of divine eternity. This idea, though, is not so clear as Carlyle's humanism. The notion of eternity is ambiguous in Carlyle's writings. Sometimes, as in *Sartor Resartus,* he tells us that only the "symbols" of religion change, while the "truths" of religion do not. At other times Carlyle highlights the flux and qualitative progress in the universe so much that the notion of "eternity" no longer fits the scheme. In a world where "everything does coöperate with all . . .no thought, word or act of man but has sprung withal out of all men, and works sooner or later, recognisably or irrecognisably, on all men," there is constant ramifying and complexifying.[13] Everything that exists or has existed still leaves its imprint on the present and future. Carlyle lived in an intellectual context that was evolutionary at its very core; and the idea of evolution is difficult to reconcile with the traditional idea of eternity. It is probably safe to assume that Carlyle never completely followed out the full consequences of the nothing-is-ever-lost philosophy, but in describing the universe in the language of flux and becoming, he has removed much of the logical underpinning for the idea of "eternity."

Carlyle's influence on traditional theology included the removal or erosion of the sense of a divine personality, omnipotence, and eternity. These elements were part of a general tendency to reduce the role that God plays in the universe. Instead of the Almighty being principal actor on the world's stage, Carlyle has put man there. Carlyle emphasizes the aggressive, active side of human nature. Man is Promethean, or Faustian, in Carlyle's view.

The Promethean aspects of human nature appear again and again in Carlyle's writings, for they are the primary qualities of human life. Whether in aesthetic theory, doctrine of labor, social views, or quest for the Hero, the will to control, to make, and to overcome is first and foremost. We are what we do; and we do because the action is a natural expression of the vital force and purposefulness in us. [14]

We cannot be passive, for life is always a struggle; and we must be canny and aggressive if we wish to live well:

> Yet nothing can be surer in this world of ours, than that he who will not struggle cannot conquer. Alas, it is a most tough obstructed wide-weltering world; wherein the stoutest swimmer is often carried far from his aim. *Ernst ist das Leben;* earnest enough! You cannot fight the battle in dressing-gown and slippers; and yet there is nothing for you but to fight,—or sit there and be butchered by Destiny. [15]

For Carlyle, the best response to the challenges of the world is to have courage and resolution. Sometimes the battle seems absurd "and yet there is nothing for you but to fight." One must affirm life by his participation in it, his grappling with its contradictions.

Concerning the process of history, some of the most important contributions Carlyle made have to do with the understanding that man is immersed in history. He cannot escape his present existence in the hope of a heavenly reward. Our destiny is worked out here on earth: "the thing thou seekest is already with thee; 'here or nowhere,' couldst thou only see!"[16] Man participates in history. He can change the character of the times by overcoming its obstacles.

Carlyle's modernity has been evident in his view of religion, human nature, and history. He was acutely sensitive to problems that are still with us nearly a century after his death in 1881. He saw the impact that technology and the city were making on human consciousness; and he recommended practical means of dealing with the changed conditions. He felt the need for authenticity in life. In his words, we must "fashion our own world," as Goethe did with an awareness of our transcendence of circumstances and with the power that comes from seeing, deciding, and acting out our own choices.

Carlyle's outlook was a mixture of optimism and pessimism that still seems modern in the twentieth century. Long before atomic bombs, heart transplants, and communications satellites, he realized the power that science had given men. He knew that we "can do." At the same time he was aware of human fallibility and the terrible misuse of resources of which we are still guilty. He felt strongly about the lack of foresight and decisiveness that we so often exhibit. Life is on the brink of the falls; we stand "at the conflux of two eternities" and yet we either miss the chance, do not care, or blunder.

Carlyle, modern Marxists, and radical theologians share many of the same understandings of God, man, and the character of the world. Carlyle does not go so far as the Marxists do in their humanism (he does not deny a supreme force exists), but he does move in the direction of reducing or eliminating God's role on earth and increasing the stress on human activity. Carlyle lived a century before what is now termed the *Marxist-Christian dialogue,* but his thinking contains some of the same elements that are now found in that dialogue.[17] The argument is not that there is direct influence from Carlyle to the conversations going on between Marxists and Christians, but that the tendencies that can be seen in mid-twentieth-century theology were presaged a century before in Carlyle's writings.

The specific points of Carlyle's modernity have their equivalents in recent writing. Of man's responsibility for himself, Charles M. Savage writes: "Modern theology wants to rid itself of the 'stop-gap-helper-god' concept. Modern theology no longer says that man is dependent on God for everything; instead it stresses man's responsibility in this world."[18] Carlyle is more pictorial, but the sentiments are the same when he tells us to put away the dressing gown and slippers or be "butchered by Destiny."

For Marx, his followers, and many Christian thinkers, the active side of human nature is primary. The universe presents us with circumstances that alienate us from God, nature, and each other, but these circumstances do not spell mortality—instead they are a stimulus, a challenge to man to stretch himself to the utmost. Pain, contradiction, even doubt, writes Carlyle, call forth our heroic instincts.

John A. T. Robinson's *Honest to God,* which is credited with marking the beginning of "radical theology," describes a trend toward "worldly holiness." "The 'beyond' (is) *in the midst of our life,* the holy (is) *in the* common."[19] One of the main thrusts of *Sartor Resartus* (1833) is precisely this belief—the infinite is revealed in the finite; the ideal is in the actual.

Roger Garaudy, reporting on the Marxist-Christian dialogue, writes: "No longer is the relationship between

God and the world a relationship of alternatives: 'either God *or* the world.' Now it is a dialectical relationship: 'God *in* the world.' "[20] Heaven and hell become metaphors for earthly experiences. The three-layered universe becomes one layered.

Human creativity and participation in historical processes is another facet of the "new theology" and of Marxism. To exist is to create. Man is the result of his own labor; and he sees himself reflected in his own work. Thought and "being" emerge out of work and action.

The radical theologians and the Marxists talk about *becoming* more than *being*. The "pull of the future" with its hope of renewal is the real focus of attention. The God of the above must yield to the God of the ahead.

> Seen in this perspective, Christianity does not rule out but actually implies militant effort turned towards the future and its construction. "As men, it is our duty to act as if there were no limits to our power. Having become, by existence, collaborators in a creation which is developing within us in such a way as will very likely lead us to an end (even earthly) which is far more exalted and far off than we think, we must help God with all our strength and so work with matter as if our salvation depended on our industry alone."[21]

There is a strong pragmatic and experimental element to radical theology and to Marxist thought. The role of theology and philosophy is to bring about fundamental changes in social institutions, not primarily to formulate theories. One must engage himself in the actualities of the world. This secularism and pragmatism is the same as that of *Past and Present* in which Carlyle feels that the church is heavy with child, full of cotton trades, factory towns, and chimney steeples. If older methods of organizing society no longer work well, we must try something new, even if it is a revolutionary change, like giving the proletariat a share in owning the means of production.

The general tendency of Carlyle's thought is right in touch with "new" theological and philosophical trends on two major themes: humanism and secularism.

Carlyle saw many things in his own times that are still issues confronting us now. He was sensitive to what he summed up as "a deep-lying struggle in the whole fabric of society; a boundless grinding collision of the New with the Old."[22] He knew that something unprecedented was happening and he made an attempt to chart new directions that would solve some of the problems presented by changed conditions. And his courage was unfailing. In meeting the fears that breaking old religious symbols might mean that the new would never come, Carlyle asserts: "That, with Superstition, Religion is also passing away, seems to us a still more ungrounded fear. Religion cannot pass away. The burning of a little straw may hide the stars of the sky; but the stars are there, and will reappear."[23] In Carlyle's sensitivity and courage lie his contribution to our understanding of ourselves and our times.

Notes

Introduction

1. James Anthony Froude, *Thomas Carlyle: A History of His Life in London, 1834–1881*, 1:248.

2. J. Hillis Miller, Jr., *The Disappearance of God*, p. 1.

3. Thomas Carlyle, *Sartor Resartus*, p. 216.

4. One of the finest recent studies of Carlyle is Albert J. LaValley's *Carlyle and the Idea of the Modern*. In it LaValley explores Carlyle's modernity in "two general forms: first, a close aesthetic study of Carlyle's writings . . . second, a comparison of Carlyle with authors more generally assumed to be 'modern' (Blake, Nietzsche, Marx, and others)," p. 1. My interests are narrower than LaValley's since the main focus is on Carlyle's modernity as it relates to his religion.

5. In emphasizing human responsibility for social destiny Carlyle places himself in the same category as Karl Marx. In fact, Marx and Engels read Carlyle and admired parts of his writings, a relationship that has yet to be explored thoroughly. LaValley's *Carlyle and the Idea of the Modern* and Phillip Rosenberg's *The Seventh Hero* explore some aspects of what Marx and Carlyle might have in common.

6. A. Abbott Ikeler in *Puritan Temper and Transcendental Faith* examines the influence of Calvinistic theories of art on Carlyle's literary vision.

7. Charles Frederick Harrold, *Carlyle and German Thought*, pp. vi–vii.

8. Charles Frederick Harrold, "The Nature of Carlyle's Calvinism," pp. 475–86.

9. Matthew Arnold, "Dover Beach," *Poetical Works*, ll. 21–37, pp. 211–12.

10. Ibid., "Empedocles on Etna," act 1, sc. 2, ll. 82–85, p. 415.

11. Edward FitzGerald, *The Rubáiyát*, quatrain 26, p. 62.

12. Alfred Lord Tennyson, "The Vision of Sin," *Tennyson's Poetry*, ll. 93–94, p. 108.

13. Matthew Arnold, "Rugby Chapel," *Poetical Works*, ll. 58-72, p. 288.

14. Alfred Lord Tennyson, "In Memoriam," *Tennyson's Poetry*, sec. 3, ll. 5–12, pp. 121–22.

15. FitzGerald, *The Rubáiyát*, quatrain 52, p. 88.

16. Arthur Hugh Clough, "Unfinished Poems," no. 21, *The Poems of Arthur Hugh Clough*, ll. 16–18, p. 409.

17. FitzGerald, *The Rubáiyát*, quatrains 32 and 33, pp. 68–69.

The Significance of Labor

1. Thomas Carlyle, *Past and Present*, 10:7, in the *Centenary Edition: The Works of Thomas Carlyle in Thirty Volumes*. Unless otherwise noted, all references to Carlyle's works are to this edition. In the case of single volumes the volume number will be that of the *Centenary Edition*. In the case of multivolume works, the volume number will be that of the original edition.

2. For example, Alfred Cobban, "Carlyle's French Revolution," p. 309.

3. Thomas Carlyle, "Biography," 3:57. *Critical and Miscellaneous Essays* occupies volumes 26 through 30 in the *Centenary Edition*.

4. Carlyle, *Past and Present*, 10:205.

5. Thomas Carlyle, *Heroes and Hero-Worship*, 5:26.

6. William Irvine, "Carlyle and T. H. Huxley," p. 115.

7. Thomas Carlyle, "Characteristics," *Critical and Miscellaneous Essays*, 3:27.

8. Carlyle, *Past and Present*, 10:263.

9. Thomas Carlyle, *The French Revolution: A History by Thomas Carlyle*, 2:124.

10. Ibid., 3:289.

11. Carlyle, *Past and Present*, 10:283.

12. Ibid., p. 281.

13. Carlyle, *Heroes and Hero-Worship*, 5:203.

14. Thomas Carlyle, *Frederick the Great*, 1:293. *Frederick the Great* occupies volumes 12 through 19 in the *Centenary Edition*.

15. Thomas Carlyle, "Signs of the Times," *Critical and Miscellaneous Essays*, 2:72.

16. Thomas Carlyle, *Sartor Resartus*, p. 55.

17. Ibid.

18. Appendix to Harrold's edition of *Sartor Resartus*, p. 317. Letter to John Sterling, 4 June 1835.

19. Carlyle, *Past and Present*, 10:91–92.

20. Irvine, "Carlyle and T. H. Huxley," p. 115.

21. Carlyle, *Sartor Resartus*, p. 162.

22. Carlyle, *Heroes and Hero-Worship*, 5:102.

23. Both quotations from "Characteristics," *Critical and Miscellaneous Essays*, 3:38–39.

24. Carlyle, *Heroes and Hero-Worship*, 5:61.

25. Ibid., p. 84.

26. Carlyle, "Characteristics," *Critical and Miscellaneous Essays*, 3:43.

27. Carlyle, *Sartor Resartus*, pp. 195–96.

28. The word *gigmanity* is explained in "Jean Paul Friedrich Richter," *Critical and Miscellaneous Essays*, 2:130. Anyone who keeps a gig is respectable.

29. Carlyle, *Sartor Resartus*, p. 190.

30. Ibid., p. 191.

31. Carlyle, *Heroes and Hero-Worship*, 5:197. Thomas Carlyle, "Legislation for Ireland," in *Rescued Essays*, pp. 83–84.

32. Carlyle read the Old Testament and was, no doubt, familiar with the prophet Amos, who uses the image of the wall and plumb line. The interpretation of the metaphor comes from Dr. John F. Priest, lecturing on Old Testament humanism.

33. Carlyle, "Characteristics," *Critical and Miscellaneous Essays*, 3:28.

34. Carlyle, *Heroes and Hero-Worship*, 5:70.

35. Thomas Carlyle, "Shooting Niagara: And After?" *Critical and Miscellaneous Essays*, 5:40.

36. Carlyle, *Past and Present*, 10:206.

37. Carlyle, *French Revolution*, 2:4.

38. Carlyle, "Ireland," *Rescued Essays*, p. 75.

39. Thomas Carlyle, *Reminiscences*, 1:4.

40. Carlyle, *Sartor Resartus*, pp. 196–97.

41. Ibid., p. 254, note 3.

42. There is direct literary influence on Marx and Engels from Carlyle's writings. In *The Condition of the Working Class in England*, Engels quotes "Chartism" enthusiastically half-a-dozen times. He shares Carlyle's concern for the starving Irish; he uses Carlyle as an authority for the statement that working Englishmen hate the immigrant Irish who compete for jobs and lower wages; and he agrees with Carlyle that the rage and frustration of the masses make England a powder keg that could blow up in a revolution. Most of all Engels admires the vivid portraits of people who callously flaunt their wealth in the face of poverty. "Carlyle gives in his *Past and Present* (London, 1843) a splendid description of the English bourgeoisie and its disgusting money-greed." Karl Marx and Frederick Engels, *Karl Marx and Frederick Engels on Britain*, p. 102.

43. Karl Marx, *Writings of the Young Marx on Philosophy and Society*, p. 266.

44. Ernst Fischer, ed., and Anna Bostock, trans., *The Essential Marx*, pp. 31–32.

45. Karl Marx, *Capital: A Critical Analysis of Capitalist Production*, 1:97.

Carlyle's Early Heroes: Men of Ideas

1. Thomas Carlyle, "Sir Walter Scott," *Critical and Miscellaneous Essays*, 4:24.

2. Thomas Carlyle, "Goethe's Works," *Critical and Miscellaneous Essays*, 2:395.

3. Thomas Carlyle, "Burns," *Critical and Miscellaneous Essays*, 1:262.

4. Ibid., p. 263.

5. Ibid., p. 265.

6. Thomas Carlyle, *Heroes and Hero-Worship*, 5:188.

7. Carlyle, "Burns," *Critical and Miscellaneous Essays*, 1:311.

8. Ibid., p. 316.

9. Thomas Carlyle, *Frederick the Great*, 3:177–78.

10. Thomas Carlyle, "Voltaire," *Critical and Miscellaneous Essays*, 1:400–401.

11. Ibid., p. 459.

12. See also "Boswell's Life of Johnson," *Critical and Miscellaneous Essays*, 3:134, where Carlyle refuses to decide whether Samuel Johnson or David Hume is more gifted.

13. Thomas Carlyle, *Early Letters of Thomas Carlyle*, 1:41.

14. Carlyle, "Sir Walter Scott," *Critical and Miscellaneous Essays*, 4:43.

15. Carlyle, "Voltaire," *Critical and Miscellaneous Essays*, 1:410.

16. Ibid., pp. 447–49.

17. Essay on Diderot follows the rough lines of Voltaire. He receives high marks for the same reasons, yet he is a "Denier."

18. Carlyle, "Boswell's Life of Johnson," *Critical and Miscellaneous Essays*, 3:90.

19. Carlyle, *Heroes and Hero-Worship*, 5:182.

20. Carlyle, "Boswell's Life of Johnson," *Critical and Miscellaneous Essays*, 3:126.

21. Thomas Carlyle, "Goethe," *Critical and Miscellaneous Essays*, 1:214.

22. Ibid., p. 203.

23. Ibid., p. 208.

24. Ibid., pp. 207–8.

25. Carlyle, "Goethe's Works," *Critical and Miscellaneous Essays*, 2:404.

26. Ibid., p. 430.

27. Carlyle, "Goethe," *Critical and Miscellaneous Essays*, 1:210.

28. Thomas Carlyle, "Death of Goethe," *Critical and Miscellaneous Essays*, 2:377.

29. Carlyle, "Goethe," *Critical and Miscellaneous Essays*, 1:208.

30. Ibid., p. 250.

31. Eric Bentley, *A Century of Hero-Worship*, p. 67.

32. Thomas Carlyle, "Mirabeau," *Critical and Miscellaneous Essays*, 3:412.

33. Ibid., p. 435.

34. Ibid., p. 469.

35. Ibid., p. 466.

36. Thomas Carlyle, *The French Revolution: A History by Thomas Carlyle*, 1:166.

37. Carlyle, "Mirabeau," *Critical and Miscellaneous Essays*, 3:453.

38. Carlyle, *French Revolution*, 1:195.

39. Carlyle, "Mirabeau," *Critical and Miscellaneous Essays*, 3:411.

40. Carlyle, "Goethe's Works," *Critical and Miscellaneous Essays,* 2:399.

41. Carlyle, *Heroes and Hero-Worship,* 5:239.

42. Ibid., p. 241.

43. Ibid., p. 7.

44. Ibid., p. 28.

45. Carlyle, *Heroes and Hero-Worship,* 5:22.

46. Ibid., pp. 30–31.

47. Ibid., pp. 28–29.

48. Ibid., p. 21.

49. Carlyle, *Heroes and Hero-Worship,* 5:69.

50. Ibid., p. 55.

51. Ibid., p. 107.

52. Ibid., p. 52.

53. Carlyle, *Heroes and Hero-Worship,* 5:45.

54. Ibid., p. 53.

55. Ibid., p. 70.

56. Ibid., p. 83.

57. Carlyle, *Heroes and Hero-Worship,* 5:92.

58. Ibid.

59. Ibid., p. 95.

60. Ibid., p. 97.

61. Carlyle, *Heroes and Hero-Worship,* 5:108.

62. Ibid., p. 101.

63. Thomas Carlyle, *Lectures on the History of Literature,* p. 147.

64. Ibid., pp. 152–53.

65. Ibid., p. 153.

66. Carlyle, *Heroes and Hero-Worship,* 5:122.

67. Ibid., p. 146.

68. Ibid., p. 148.

69. Ibid., p. 158.

70. Carlyle, *Heroes and Hero-Worship,* 5:162.

71. Ibid., p. 182.

72. Ibid., p. 184.

73. Ibid., p. 185.

74. Ibid.

75. Carlyle, "Goethe," *Critical and Miscellaneous Essays,* 1:210.

76. Carlyle, *Heroes and Hero-Worship,* 5:115.

Carlyle's Later Heroes: Men of Action

1. Thomas Carlyle, *Heroes and Hero-Worship,* 5:196.

2. Ibid., p. 209.

3. Thomas Carlyle, *Cromwell,* 1:412. *Cromwell* occupies volumes 6 through 9 of the *Centenary Edition.*

4. Ibid., 3:80.

5. Ibid., 3:194.

6. Thomas Carlyle, "Mirabeau," *Critical and Miscellaneous Essays,* 3:405–6.

7. Carlyle, *Heroes and Hero-Worship*, 5:217.

8. Thomas Carlyle, *Sartor Resartus*, p. 31.

9. Ibid., p. 32.

10. Compare Carlyle's attraction-repulsion attitude toward Diderot, Voltaire, and Hume. Carlyle himself is often a skeptic and is attracted to Hume by his caustic questioning.

11. Carlyle, *Cromwell*, 2:226–27.

12. Ibid., 4:179.

13. Ibid., 1:12.

14. Thomas Carlyle, *Frederick the Great*, 3:308.

15. Ibid., 1:14.

16. Ibid., 1:17.

17. Ibid., 3:193.

18. For a discussion of events of Frederick's first week as king see Carlyle, *Frederick the Great*, 3:278–93.

19. Ibid., 1:14.

20. Eric Bentley, *A Century of Hero-Worship*, pp. 53–58, and Albert J. LaValley, *Carlyle and the Idea of the Modern*, pp. 264–78, have excellent discussions of Carlyle's *Frederick the Great*.

21. Carlyle, *Frederick the Great*, 1:293.

22. Nancy Mitford, "Tam and Fritz: Carlyle and Frederick the Great," p. 5.

23. Carlyle, *Frederick the Great*, 2:366–67.

24. Ibid., 2:406.

25. Bentley, *A Century of Hero-Worship*, p. 54, quoted from *Frederick the Great*.

26. Ibid., p. 239.

27. Thomas Carlyle, "The Nigger Question," *Critical and Miscellaneous Essays*, 4:356.

28. Thomas Carlyle, *Past and Present*, 10:212.

29. Feodor Dostoevski, *The Brothers Karamazov*, p. 267.

Eschatology and Social Theory

1. Hill Shine, *Carlyle and the Saint-Simonians*.

2. René Wellek, "Carlyle and the Philosophy of History."

3. Thomas Carlyle, *Heroes and Hero-Worship*, 5:78.

4. Thomas Carlyle, *Lectures on the History of Literature*, p. 21.

5. Ibid., p. 35.

6. Thomas Carlyle, "Historic Survey of German Poetry," *Critical and Miscellaneous Essays*, 2:342.

7. Carlyle, "Jean Paul Friedrich Richter," *Critical and Miscellaneous Essays*, 1:19.

8. Thomas Carlyle, *The French Revolution: A History by Thomas Carlyle*, 1:226.

9. Carlyle, *Lectures on the History of Literature*, p. 124.

10. Thomas Carlyle, "Characteristics," *Critical and Miscellaneous Essays*, 3:37.

11. Ibid., pp. 32, 37, respectively.

12. Thomas Carlyle, *Past and Present,* 10:276.

13. Carlyle, "Characteristics," *Critical and Miscellaneous Essays,* 3:26.

14. Thomas Carlyle, "On History," *Critical and Miscellaneous Essays,* 2:88.

15. Carlyle, "Characteristics," *Critical and Miscellaneous Essays,* 3:38.

16. Hill Shine, *Carlyle's Fusion of Poetry, History, and Religion by 1834,* p. 19. See Thomas Carlyle, trans., *Wilhelm Meister,* 1:29.

17. Carlyle, *Heroes and Hero-Worship,* 5:118.

18. Carlyle, *Lectures on the History of Literature,* p. 99.

19. Carlyle, "Characteristics," *Critical and Miscellaneous Essays,* 3:30.

20. Thomas Carlyle, "Signs of the Times," *Critical and Miscellaneous Essays,* 2:57.

21. Wellek, "Carlyle and the Philosophy of History," p. 58.

22. Eric Bentley, *A Century of Hero-Worship,* p. 166.

23. Carlyle, "Characteristics," *Critical and Miscellaneous Essays,* 3:43.

24. Carlyle, *Past and Present,* 10:248–49.

25. See Carlyle, "Signs of the Times," *Critical and Miscellaneous Essays,* 2:64–65, for empiricism.

26. Ibid., p. 74.

27. Ibid., pp. 76–77.

28. Thomas Carlyle, "Jesuitism," *Latter-Day Pamphlets,* 20:316–18.

29. Carlyle, *Past and Present,* 10:287.

30. Ibid., p. 275.

31. Ibid., p. 266.

32. Ibid.

33. Ibid., p. 271.

34. Thomas Carlyle, "Chartism," *Critical and Miscellaneous Essays,* 4:127.

35. Carlyle, *Past and Present,* 10:281–82.

36. Ibid., p. 264.

37. Ibid., p. 265.

38. Ibid.

39. Carlyle, *Past and Present,* p. 267.

40. Ibid., p. 76.

41. Ibid., p. 34.

42. Ibid., p. 256.

43. Frederick William Roe, *The Social Philosophy of Carlyle and Ruskin,* p. 323.

44. Carlyle, *Past and Present,* 10:296–98.

45. Thomas Carlyle, *Rescued Essays,* pp. 78–79.

46. Thomas Carlyle, *Sartor Resartus,* note 1, p. 128, cites four uses of time as it appears in *Sartor Resartus:* (1) as a symbol of evil and destruction; (2) as a symbol of revelation; (3) as opportu-

nity; (4) as a prison that shuts us out from the truth of eternity.

47. Carlyle, *Lectures on the History of Literature*, p. 64.

48. Thomas Carlyle, "The Present Time," *Latter-Day Pamphlets*, 20:46.

49. Ibid., p. 245.

50. James Anthony Froude, *Thomas Carlyle: A History of His Life in London, 1834-1881*, 1:324.

51. Ibid., 2:18.

Conclusion

1. Thomas Carlyle, *Letters of Thomas Carlyle, 1826–1836*, 2 April 1828, 1:142.

2. Ibid., January 1831, 1:254.

3. Ibid., 10 October 1830, 1:234, and 18 February 1832, 2:23.

4. James Anthony Froude, *Thomas Carlyle: A History of His Life in London, 1834–1881*, 1:38.

5. Ibid., pp. 33–34.

6. Carlyle, *Letters of Thomas Carlyle, 1826–1836*, 21 October 1838, 2:382.

7. Thomas Carlyle, *Letters of Thomas Carlyle to John Stuart Mill, John Sterling, and Robert Browning*, 20 January 1834, p. 95.

8. Carlyle, *Letters of Thomas Carlyle, 1826–1836*, 8 January 1833, 2:79.

9. James Anthony Froude, *Thomas Carlyle: A History of the First Forty Years of His Life, 1795–1835*, 2:2.

10. Carlyle, *Letters of Thomas Carlyle to John Stuart Mill, John Sterling, and Robert Browning*, 4 June 1835, p. 194.

11. Both quotations are from Thomas Carlyle, *Reminiscences*, 2:206.

12. Thomas Carlyle, "Goethe," *Critical and Miscellaneous Essays*, 1:251.

13. Thomas Carlyle, *Heroes and Hero-Worship*, 5:102.

14. See Carlyle, *Heroes and Hero-Worship*, 5:106–7, where vital force is what makes us essentially human.

15. Carlyle, *Letters of Thomas Carlyle to John Stuart Mill, John Sterling, and Robert Browning*, 19 November 1832, p. 24.

16. Thomas Carlyle, *Sartor Resartus*, p. 197.

17. One wonders what the relation of Calvinism proper (meaning John Calvin) is to a secular ideology like that of Karl Marx. Why did Calvin's stress on Almighty God lead to such a will to work on earth, saving money and so forth? Max Weber's *The Protestant Ethic and the Spirit of Capitalism* shows an intriguing aspect of the whole relationship between Calvinism and the secularism that both the capitalists and the Marxists share.

18. Charles M. Savage, "Opium or Leaven?" p. 110.

19. John A. T. Robinson, *Honest to God*, p. 86.

20. Roger A. Garaudy, *From Anathema to Dialogue*, p. 46.

21. Ibid., p. 54. Quoted from Teilhard de Chardin, "Christology and Evolution."

22. Thomas Carlyle, "Signs of the Times," *Critical and Miscellaneous Essays*, 2:82.

23. Thomas Carlyle, "Voltaire," *Critical and Miscellaneous Essays*, 1:468.

Bibliography

Books

Arnold, Matthew. *Poetical Works*. Edited by C. B. Tinker and H. F. Lowry. London: Oxford University Press, 1950.

Bentley, Eric. *A Century of Hero-Worship*. 2d ed. Boston: Beacon Press, Inc., 1957.

Carlyle, Thomas. *Centenary Edition: The Works of Thomas Carlyle in Thirty Volumes*. Edited by H. D. Traill. 30 vols. New York: Charles Scribner's Sons, N.D.

———. *Early Letters of Thomas Carlyle*. Edited by Charles Eliot Norton. 2 vols. London: Macmillan, 1886.

———. *The French Revolution: A History by Thomas Carlyle*. Edited by J. Holland Rose. 3 vols. London: G. Bell and Sons, 1915.

———. *Lectures on the History of Literature*. Edited by J. Reay Greene. London: Ellis and Elvey, 1892.

———. *Letters of Thomas Carlyle, 1826–1836*. Edited by Charles Eliot Norton. 2 vols. London: Macmillan, 1888.

———. *Letters of Thomas Carlyle to John Stuart Mill, John Sterling, and Robert Browning*. Edited by Alexander Carlyle. New York: Frederick A. Stokes, 1923.

———. *Reminiscences*. Edited by Charles Eliot Norton. 2 vols. London: Macmillan, 1887.

———. *Rescued Essays*. Edited by Percy Newberry. New York: Charles Scribner's Sons, 1892.

———. *Sartor Resartus*. Edited by Charles Frederick Harrold. New York: Odyssey Press, 1937.

Clough, Arthur Hugh. *The Poems of Arthur Hugh Clough*. Edited by H. F. Lowry, A. L. P. Norrington, and F. L. Mulhauser. London: Clarendon Press, 1951.

Dostoevsky, Fyodor. *The Brothers Karamazov*. Translated by Constance Garnett. New York: Macmillan, 1916.

Fischer, Ernst, ed., and Bostock, Anna, trans. *The Essential Marx*. New York: Herder & Herder, 1970.

FitzGerald, Edward. *The Rubáiyát*. Edited by Carl J. Weber. Waterville, Maine: Colby College Press, 1959.

Froude, James Anthony. *Thomas Carlyle: A History of the First Forty Years of His Life, 1795-1835*. 2 vols. New York: Charles Scribner's Sons, 1882.

———. *Thomas Carlyle: A History of His Life in London, 1834–1881*. 2 vols. New York: Charles Scribner's Sons, 1884.

Garaudy, Roger A. *From Anathema to Dialogue*. Translated by Luke O'Neill. New York: Herder & Herder, 1966.

Harrold, Charles Frederick. *Carlyle and German Thought*. New Haven: Yale University Press, 1934.

Ikeler, A. Abbott. *Puritan Temper and Transcendental Faith*. Columbus: Ohio State University Press, 1972.

LaValley, Albert J. *Carlyle and the Idea of the Modern*. New Haven: Yale University Press, 1968.

Marx, Karl. *Capital: A Critical Analysis of Capitalist Production*. Edited by Frederick Engels, and translated by Samuel Moore and Edward Aveling. New York: Humboldt Publishing Company (1886).

———. *Writings of the Young Marx on Philosophy and Society*. Translated and edited by Loyd D. Easton and Kurt H. Guddat. New York: Doubleday & Company, Inc., 1967.

Marx, Karl, and Engels, Frederick. *Karl Marx and Frederick Engels on Britain*. Edition prepared by the Marx-Engels-Lenin-Stalin Institute of the Central Committee. Moscow: Foreign Language Publishing House, 1953.

Miller, J. Hillis, Jr. *The Disappearance of God*. Cambridge, Mass.: Belknap Press of Harvard University Press, 1963.

Robinson, John A. T. *Honest to God*. Philadelphia: Westminster Press, 1963.

Roe, Frederick William. *The Social Philosophy of Carlyle and Ruskin*. New York: Harcourt and Brace, 1921.

Rosenberg, Phillip. *The Seventh Hero*. Cambridge: Harvard University Press, 1975.

Shine, Hill. *Carlyle and the Saint-Simonians*. Baltimore: Johns Hopkins Press, 1941.

———. *Carlyle's Fusion of Poetry, History, and Religion by 1834*. Port Washington, New York: Kennikat Press, 1938.

Tennyson, Alfred Lord. *Tennyson's Poetry*. Edited by Robert W. Hill. New York: W. W. Norton & Company, Inc., 1971.

Weber, Max. *The Protestant Ethic and the Spirit of Capitalism*. Translated by Talcott Parsons. New York: Charles Scribner's Sons, 1958.

Articles and Essays

Cobban, Alfred. "Carlyle's French Revolution." *History* 48 (October 1963):303–16.

Goodwin, Charles J. "Carlyle's Ethics." *International Journal of Ethics* 15 (1904–1905):198–210.

Harrold, Charles Frederick. "The Nature of Carlyle's Calvinism." *Studies in Philology* 33 (July 1936):475–86.

Irvine, William. "Carlyle and T. H. Huxley," in *Booker Memorial Studies*. Edited by Hill Shine. Chapel Hill: University of North Carolina Press, 1950.

Mitford, Nancy. "Tam and Fritz: Carlyle and Frederick the Great." *History Today* 18 (January 1968):3–13.

Savage, Charles M. "Opium or Leaven?" in *The Christian-Marxist Dialogue.* Edited by Paul Oestreicher. London: Collier-Macmillan, 1969.

Wellek, René. "Carlyle and the Philosophy of History." *Philological Quarterly* 23 (January 1944):55–76.

Index